I0813424

DEFY GRAVITY

CEDRIC DUMONT

How to break free from boundaries and limiting beliefs

Lannoo
Campus

D/2025/45/270 – ISBN 978-90-209-8676-1 – NUR 800

Cover design: Wendy De Haes
Interior design: Keppie & Keppie
Translation: Ingrid Van Waes

LannooCampus Publishers is a subsidiary of Lannoo Publishers, the book and multimedia division of Lannoo Publishers nv.

LannooCampus Publishers
Vaartkom 41 box 01.02
3000 Leuven
Belgium

P.O. Box 23202
1100 DS Amsterdam
The Netherlands

www.lannoocampus.com

Contents

Elevate your consciousness to reclaim your life.

The things that hold us back

Are you addicted to comfort and unwilling to change? Then this book isn't for you. If you're hooked on instant gratification, this book won't do you any good either—unless you want to free yourself from that urge. If you want to look back with regret at all the things you didn't do, then this book isn't for you. You'd be better off reading something that reinforces your doubts and keeps you safely away from bold choices. Regret over missed opportunities is the price you pay for your desire for certainty. That's the price tag of regret: only when it's too late do you realise you haven't followed the path you truly wanted.

In my first book, 'Dare to jump', I wrote about building up courage and daring to take action. How do you deal with fear? How do you develop the skills needed to take that daring leap? It was about cultivating the right mindset—breaking through limiting beliefs and daring to dream big. In this new book, I invite you into my laboratory for high-stakes dream making. To make our dreams come true and rise above ourselves, we must focus on five key points:

1. We know the path but don't follow it.
2. Mental obstacles hold us back.
3. Aggressive comfort makes us weak.
4. Pleasure is not the same as fulfilment.
5. Dare to challenge yourself.

The traits and skills needed to achieve your goals are not some well-kept secret. That information can be found in hundreds of books and thousands of articles. Anyone who's been paying attention knows the way. So why don't we follow it? Why do we fail to make progress? What causes us to stray, keeping us from ever reaching our goals?

Everyone knows how to lose weight, yet actually starting—let alone sticking with it—is incredibly difficult. Every smoker knows smoking is bad for their health, yet they keep lighting up those cancer sticks. We know the way to more and better, but we don't take it. Often, we don't do what we want or need to do because mental obstacles hold us back. Most of the time, we aren't even aware of them—they exist in our subconscious. Many behaviours are deeply ingrained, whether through our genes or our upbringing.

Why are so many people afraid of those who speak a different language or have a different skin colour? Because we instinctively trust people who look and speak like us, while seeing outsiders as a potential threat to our own tribe. Even people in our own country who dress differently from the norm can make us suspicious. And we, too, fear social judgement: the fear of being cast out of the group is powerful. In prehistoric times, that meant death. Without your tribe, survival was much harder.

Today, we still feel the need to belong to a group, but we no longer have to fight a real survival battle. Ironically, it's not scarcity but an overdose of comfort that's killing us. In the case of lifestyle diseases, this is quite literally true. In our comfortable environment, we live with a lack of intention. As much as 95 percent of what we do and think happens on autopilot. We no longer need to make an effort to survive, so we end up being lived. Only when you make conscious choices do you regain control over your own life.

Ironically, all our modern comfort does not bring peace of mind. Since 1987, depression and anxiety disorders have increased by 400 to 500 percent. Is this increase because we're more open about mental health, or are these conditions truly on the rise? Either way, there is now a lot of attention given to mental health and emotional well-being. It is a good thing that mental health problems can be discussed openly. At the same time, I believe that this focus on mental well-being actually increases anxiety. After all, mental well-being is not achieved by avoiding all possible problems but by learning to deal with them in the right way.

I am convinced that excessive comfort does not make people happy. If you're never challenged and never dare to step outside your comfort zone, you become a slave to your need for control. You want certainty at all times, in all situations, shielding yourself from every possible risk. But the result isn't greater peace of mind—it's actually more anxiety. Do I really have everything under control, or will unexpected surprises still arise? Human evolution didn't take place in a safe, controlled environment—danger could appear at any time, anywhere. Ultimately, as humans, we are primarily programmed to survive and reproduce. The rest, genetically speaking, is of secondary importance. All our dreams, ambitions, and creative drives are merely side effects.

Our brains are adapted to surviving in the wilderness, not to the endless comfort with which Western society surrounds itself. That's why I believe a healthy dose of stress is actually good for our mental well-being. A little pressure makes us more resilient. However, many people go so far in their pursuit of mental peace that they can no longer handle negative feedback or setbacks. Every minor conflict feels like a catastrophic upheaval. Companies are already noticing how young employees quit at the slightest conflict, seemingly because they can't handle rejection. But rejection is simply part of life. The problem isn't rejection itself—it's our relentless craving for comfort. That's why I call it aggressive comfort.

I truly believe that a bit of stress is necessary to be productive and creative. Challenges force you to push yourself further. A company or society without challenge doesn't work. Such an organisation lulls itself to sleep or gets pushed aside by more assertive competitors.

Disruption is the new normal. In 2020, COVID-19 spread across the globe, and the entire planet went into lockdown—a world first. We had never experienced anything like it. Once the worst waves of the pandemic subsided, the conflict in Ukraine erupted. Energy prices skyrocketed, and inflation eroded the purchasing power of many households. The economy struggled to stay afloat. Meanwhile, violence flared up again in the Middle East. Suddenly, we were living from one crisis to the next.

Are you longing for the calm waters of the past? Hate to pop your comfort balloon, but the world is not peaceful. It never was. The world is volatile, complex, and uncertain. In Western Europe, we may have briefly indulged in the illusion of stability, but it didn't last long. There's no point in hoping things will return to the way they used to be—because even in the past, we simply lived from one crisis to the next. Crisis isn't the exception—it's the rule. War, economic downturns, pandemics, disruptive technological developments like artificial intelligence—new threats are constantly emerging. There's no use in being startled every time. The real question is: how do you deal with it? How do you adapt to new circumstances?

Let's take it a step further. Adapting deserves credit, but you don't just want to survive—you want to achieve something. It's not our circumstances that hold us back from making our dreams come true; it's how we respond to them. The things that keep us from moving forward exist mostly in our minds. That's why it's important to name them. Maybe you'll recognise some of these roadblocks in your own life:

- Lack of accountability
- Limiting beliefs
- Fear of failure
- Outdated social norms
- Insecurity

- Lack of consistency
- Complacency

Obstacles like these prevent you from walking your own path. However, as you'll come to see, the most difficult path can also bring the greatest sense of fulfilment. Realising your full potential is a lifelong journey, not a quick trip you can just complete. There is no point where you'll say, 'Now I've achieved everything'. No, the road twists and turns endlessly, and the most important thing is that you keep growing.

The goal is to become so good at what you do that no one can ignore you. That's what this book is about. Countless obstacles will stand in the way of your progress. The key is to recognise and understand them—only then can you overcome them. That's why, in this book, I take a deeper look at the types of obstacles you'll encounter on your path and how they hinder your personal growth. The good news? Overcoming an obstacle helps you grow.

'What doesn't kill you makes you stronger' is a massive cliché—and often, it's simply not true. People with post-traumatic stress disorder, for example, don't feel stronger. But if an intense experience doesn't leave you traumatised, it can make you stronger. Failure isn't that big of a deal—you die a little inside, but then you get back up. And in the end, you're going to die for real someday anyway, so why be afraid of only dying a little? Slam into a wall, acknowledge your failure, and pull yourself back up.

I personally practice a dangerous discipline: base jumping. I've seen people get injured. I've even lost friends. Each time, it's a shock. But at the same time, experiencing something like that teaches you to put things into perspective. That's the biggest lesson my sport has taught me—how to see the bigger picture and keep things in perspective. It keeps me connected to my own mortality.

Seeing problems as challenges and turning risks into opportunities—yes, it sounds like empty corporate jargon, but that's what it comes down to. Hiding in your comfort zone won't make fear disappear. Step out into the world instead and discover your own path. If this mindset works in the extreme environment of my sport, where the smallest mistake can cost you your life, then you can apply it just as well in an everyday setting.

I'm taking you on a personal and practical journey through the largely unexplored territory of peak performance and optimal consciousness. If you're not yet familiar with the concepts of peak performance and flow hacking, I strongly recommend reading my first book as well. Come, let's embark on our journey. I want to show you that living in uncertain times is nothing to fear. In fact, there is a powerful connection between discomfort, growth, fulfilment, and happiness. To give you a glimpse of what's ahead: discomfort makes you happier than you think. It leads to a deep sense of fulfilment in your life.

Don't let your thoughts or your environment drag you down. Rise above it all—defy gravity.

Cedric Dumont
Summer 2025

1

The aggressive danger of comfort

Get comfortable with being uncomfortable!

The modern comfort we enjoy today is our greatest source of problems. In our pursuit of comfort, we seek physical ease and avoid unpleasant situations. Unfortunately, we are doing ourselves no favours. In fact, there is a strong correlation between comfort and depression, anxiety disorders, cardiovascular disease, obesity, and cancer. Comfort is more dangerous than the imaginary threats we fear so much.

It's new experiences that actually improve our mental well-being. Challenges, no matter how difficult, keep both our bodies and minds fit and sharp. For thousands of years, every new day was a challenge for humans. As a species, we evolved to survive in a hostile world, and you can still see this today when war breaks out. In Ukraine, people paradoxically felt happier after the Russian invasion than they did before. During wartime, the number of depression cases actually drops by 40 percent. The explanation? We are wired to confront challenges.

After the 9/11 attacks, the happiness levels of Americans also rose. That may sound shocking, and to be clear, I am not advocating bloodshed to boost global happiness. But the fact remains: a major event tends to have a positive rather than a negative effect on our well-being.

The attack on the World Trade Center in New York brought the United States together. Americans suddenly felt a deep connection with one another. 'We are one people, we are united, and we will support each other,' was the prevailing sentiment.

Such a deep connection generates an intense feeling of happiness. You feel united with your people, bound by shared values. You become part of something greater than yourself.

Our nomadic ancestors had to search for food and shelter every waking moment. Only relatively recently did humans settle into permanent communities and experience comfort. We built shelters that lasted, and with the advent of agriculture, we always had food at hand. With technological advancements, our comfort only grew. And now, in 2025, we spend most of our days sitting comfortably in a chair. Because we don't move enough, we pay for gym memberships and fitness programmes to compensate for an entire day of sitting. It sounds almost too absurd to believe, yet it's the harsh reality.

In some ways, life has become easier, but all that comfort is turning against us. Yet, despite all this comfort, we're not exactly jumping for joy. The number of burnout cases rises every year. More people are anxious and depressed than ever before. Since 1987, when the U.S. Food & Drug Administration (FDA) approved the antidepressant Prozac®, the rate of depression in the U.S. has increased by 400 percent.

Other prosperity-related diseases are also on the rise. For example, Alzheimer's diagnoses are expected to triple compared to current levels. What's driving this increase? Part of the explanation lies in our sugar-laden, high-fat diet—excess weight is harmful to the brain as well. A grim reality, considering that 70 percent of men are overweight. Thirty percent are even classified as obese. Additionally, half of the Western population now has diabetes or is in a pre-diabetic stage.

We cannot separate the rise of neurological and mental disorders from our lifestyle; the two are interconnected. Our comfortable way of life is proving to be extremely unhealthy in many ways. The solution? Step outside your comfort zone more often. A little discomfort actually leads to greater fulfilment.

A positive mind in an uncertain world

Despite all our comforts, the world is still dangerous and unstable. Pretending otherwise won't change that. But don't focus on it too much. If you only look at the negative and the threats around you,

you risk paralysing yourself. You'll retreat even deeper into your comfort zone.

COVID, Ukraine, Gaza—we seem to be stumbling from one crisis to the next. What happened to our peaceful, steady existence? Disruption has suddenly become the new normal. And while we're still processing today's shocks, artificial intelligence is looming larger on the horizon. Whose job will be safe tomorrow? The algorithms will replace us! Is there anything AI won't be able to do? How can we, as humans, still make a difference? Can you become so good at what you do that no one can ignore you?

There's another way to look at it. Perhaps artificial intelligence will create new jobs and steer the economy in a different direction. AI could just as easily simplify your work rather than make it obsolete. Maybe it's more of an ally than a threat.

Ask yourself: How are you making a difference today? Through your skills, your mindset, and your courage? That will always be the case. The demand for creative minds will never disappear. Emotional intelligence, too, will always be highly valued.

Geertrui Mieke De Ketelaere, Director of Artificial Intelligence at the research centre Imec, points out that current AI models lack context and have no overarching story to tell. That's something humans can do. So how do you make a difference? By reading a book, for instance—maybe even this book—and drawing valuable lessons from it.

However, when you watch the news, it's all too easy to lose hope. The world is doomed anyway—why even bother with something positive? Doomscrolling is incredibly tempting when the television news shapes your worldview. Our human brain seems hardwired to see everything through a negative lens. Once you start down that path, you only notice what could go wrong. And suddenly, you see that a lot can go wrong.

Our brains aren't tuned to opportunities—they're wired for threats. But once you understand that, you can counteract it. Start by turning off the TV and ignoring news websites. I am fully aware that we're living from crisis to crisis, but I avoid the news at all costs. Precisely because you have no control over all these large and small disasters, there is no point in keeping up with the news.

By definition, the news is overwhelmingly negative—it's about wars, diseases, and economic downturns. Throw in some traffic accidents, political deadlocks, and the occasional murder, and there you have it. If I asked you to name three negative news stories from the past year, you could probably rattle them off instantly. Easy. But positive news? Wait, was there any positive news at all?

All that bad news makes you feel like a mere pawn in the hands of powerful institutions and global forces. It convinces you that your own actions don't matter. And that kind of thinking is convenient—it allows you to blame external factors for everything that happens in your life, things you supposedly have no control over. You push yourself into the role of a victim and attribute your own problems to external causes.

Newsrooms, of course, know that bad news sells—it grabs the attention of viewers and readers. For our brains, negativity is irresistible. Neuroscientists have found that our minds pick up on bad news far more easily than good news. We are constantly asking ourselves: What could go wrong?

Neuroscience is quite clear on how the brain works: our brains are not built for success. A winning mentality does not come naturally to us. We are survivors, and in order to survive, we must focus primarily on threats. This principle is known as the negativity bias: we fixate on potential problems, obstacles, and dangers.

The majority of our brain has not significantly evolved since prehistoric times, meaning its core function remains the same: survival. Our prehistoric ancestors had to be constantly alert to predators, natural disasters, and hostile tribes. They needed to quickly recognise and react to threats. That instinct increased their chances of survival.

That negativity bias is still deeply embedded in our brains today. Unfortunately, we also turn that negative lens inward. Negative experiences and emotions tend to have a much greater impact than positive ones. This is why you vividly remember bad experiences but tend to forget good ones more easily. It's also why we are more sensitive to criticism than to praise—I could receive twenty positive reviews of this book, but it's that one negative comment that will keep replaying in my mind.

Imagine I receive a compliment for something I've done.

'Wow, you're really good at that,' a friend tells me.

'Thanks!' I reply. But in my head, I think, I already know I'm good at that. And so, the compliment just slides right off me.

But my friend isn't done talking yet.

'That last book of yours, though, Cedric... Pff, it was such a tough read. I'm not saying it was complete nonsense, but I just couldn't get through it.'

Now that comment sticks to my brain like Velcro. We invest far more energy in negative feedback and emotions. Criticism keeps spinning in our minds. Why did they say that? Were they trying to take me down, or was my book really that badly written?

Every day, we experience about 40 percent positive emotions and 60 percent negative ones. And we pay much more attention to the negative ones, while positive emotions are seen as normal and therefore unremarkable. You had a great meal? Sure, that's nice, but that's how it's meant to be. But if you're served overcooked pasta or sour soup, you'll still be irritated about it an hour later. That may not sound very uplifting—if you'll excuse my terribly downbeat phrasing.

In our brain, there are two areas responsible for processing emotions: the limbic system and the amygdala. The amygdala reacts most strongly to negative emotions, particularly anger and fear. These are also the most powerful emotions because they help us survive. Without fear, we wouldn't be here—our ancestors would have walked straight into danger. This explains why we experience negative emotions so much more intensely and for a longer period of time.

Elite athletes struggle far more with losing than they celebrate winning. And yet, a victory is not normal—it's what every athlete strives for. No athlete gives their all while expecting to lose; that kind of mindset wouldn't motivate anyone. But there will always be more losers than winners. The disappointment of losing lingers far longer than the thrill of victory. And if you don't learn to process that disappointment, you won't be able to move forward.

When I'm about to jump in my sport, I always hear two voices in my head. One voice lists everything that could go wrong and the terrible consequences that might follow. The other voice reassures me: 'You can do this. You've prepared well, you've trained, and you're completely focused. You're ready, so go ahead and jump.'

Because of our negativity bias, it's much easier to listen to that first voice. But if you want to live consciously, you also have to listen to the second voice so that you can make the right decision at the right moment.

Fortunately, you don't just have to accept this negativity bias—there are strategies to train your brain to think more positively. Our brains have a remarkable ability to adapt. Through conscious effort and practice, you can train yourself to focus more on positive experiences. This rewires your brain in a more positive way and makes you more resilient. This ability of the brain to adapt to changing circumstances is known as neuroplasticity.

Focusing on the positive is a habit that requires practice. It takes time, effort, and attention to train your brain, but thanks to neuroplasticity, that effort truly pays off.

Neuroplasticity: the brain in motion

Neuroplasticity is the brain's ability to adapt throughout life. The brain reorganises itself by strengthening or breaking down neural connections and forming new ones. This not only changes how the brain functions, but also alters its structure. These structural changes lay the foundation for long-term shifts in how our brain processes information.

Neuroplasticity is essential when learning new skills. Under the influence of new experiences, the brain undergoes specific changes. Through repeated exposure or practice, the relevant neural networks become more efficient, leading to improved performance.

Neuroplasticity challenges the traditional view of the brain as a fixed, unchangeable organ. The brain is a dynamic system that can function differently over the course of your life. Neuroplasticity occurs at all ages, from early childhood to old age. However, it does decline with ageing. Children are highly neuroplastic, quickly picking up new skills, adapting easily, and recovering faster. Their brains are still very malleable. But even as an adult, you can shape your brain—if you choose to.

Neuroplasticity implies that you can learn new things and continue to develop cognitively. Since neuroplasticity continues beyond childhood, lifelong learning is possible—if you keep challenging your brain with new experiences. You are never too old to learn—your brain remains adaptable even in old age.

This ability is most striking in cases of brain injury. Some people manage to regain lost skills or develop alternative abilities to compensate for the damage. Think of individuals who become blind but learn to navigate their surroundings using their hearing. That, too, is a form of learning.

As we gain a better understanding of the mechanisms behind neuroplasticity, we can apply them to enhance cognitive abilities. Engaging in complex mental tasks or taking up a new hobby challenges the brain, stimulating neuroplastic changes that strengthen cognitive functions.

Is neuroplasticity limitless? No. Neuroplasticity will not completely reset your brain—you will, to some extent, always remain yourself. Additionally, new research suggests that our lifestyle influences how strongly or weakly neuroplasticity occurs. Regular exercise, a healthy diet, good sleep, and an active social life all enhance neuroplasticity. A healthy lifestyle stimulates neurogenesis and strengthens neural connections. Conversely, an unhealthy lifestyle keeps us trapped in harmful patterns.

Neuroplasticity proves that it's never too late to change. You can always change. Nothing is set in stone—you can become the best version of yourself.

Why comfort is so dangerous

Comfort makes life easier and more pleasant. But an excessive focus on comfort can actually make us feel miserable and even unhappy. It's a strange paradox—how can physical comfort lead to mental discomfort? There are five reasons for this:

1 **Lack of challenge and growth.** When you constantly seek comfort and avoid challenging situations, you deny yourself the opportunity to grow and develop. Personal growth usually happens when we step outside our comfort zone, gain new experiences, take risks, and overcome obstacles. Without challenges, we make no progress. We feel unfulfilled and lack a sense of purpose.
2 **Reduced resilience.** Constant comfort often leads to a lack of resilience—you struggle to deal with setbacks. When you always shield yourself from discomfort, even minor difficulties can feel overwhelming. Yet, resistance and discomfort

build resilience and help you adapt to new challenges, allowing you to bounce back more quickly.

3 **Unrealistic expectations.** A strong emphasis on comfort creates unrealistic expectations about life. You start to believe that everything should always be easy, enjoyable, and instantly gratifying. When reality falls short, you end up feeling disappointed and frustrated. You don't experience true fulfilment.
4 **Diminished appreciation.** Excessive comfort makes it harder to appreciate life's small pleasures and moments of happiness. Once you get used to a certain level of comfort, you take it for granted—and no longer derive the same joy from it. As a result, you constantly chase more comfort, always pursuing the next thing that promises happiness, without truly enjoying what you already have and already do.
5 **Lack of meaningful connection.** Relying too much on comfort and convenience prevents us from forming deep, meaningful bonds with others. Strong relationships often require effort and vulnerability—both of which take us outside our comfort zone. By avoiding discomfort, you miss the chance to build deep connections with others. And in doing so, you forgo the richness of close relationships, something that all humans fundamentally need.

For the sake of clarity: striving for a certain level of comfort and convenience is not necessarily a bad thing. You don't have to sit on a hard wooden bench staring at a black-and-white television. Comfort only becomes problematic when it controls your life—when it prevents you from growing, building resilience, and experiencing life on a deeper level. A healthy balance between comfort and challenge is crucial for our overall well-being and sense of happiness.

We did not evolve for comfort

The comfortable life we lead in the Western world is the primary cause of many modern ailments: obesity, cardiovascular disease, depression, anxiety disorders, and even dementia. Abundance and comfort bring us nothing but misery. If we want to feel good, we need physical challenges and uncomfortable experiences.

We simply did not evolve for the comfortable society we live in today. For hundreds of thousands of years, every new morning brought the same challenge: survival. Making it to the next sunrise in one piece was a victory in itself. Our ancestors spent nearly every waking moment searching for food and shelter. For tens of thousands of years, humans lived this way, constantly glancing over their shoulders to check for danger. The first permanent settlements only appeared a few thousand years ago. That's when humans first experienced the kind of comfort we now take for granted—a safe place to live and a stable food supply. Suddenly, life was no longer a struggle, but merely a task.

Since then, our lives have only become easier. We no longer have to spend entire days manually plowing fields to feed our families. And yet, life remains a struggle—though now, primarily a mental one. Despite all our modern comforts, we have not become happier. In fact, it seems that more people than ever are suffering from stress and depression.

Humans have an inherent tendency to seek comfort, but today's overabundance of comfort is not good for us. We no longer face real threats in our environment, yet our brains remain just as vigilant for danger. The more physical comfort we have, the more restless our minds become. The physical struggle for survival has been replaced by a mental struggle, as seen in the rising cases of anxiety disorders and burnout. Those who try to calm their minds through excessive eating, alcohol consumption, or mindlessly scrolling social media often find themselves feeling even more restless.

Some anthropologists speculate that thousands of years ago, when humans still roamed the wilderness as nomads, we were actually happier. Our needs were easily met—we required little more than food and water, shelter from the elements, and the security of our tribe. We existed in a natural state of mindfulness, living entirely in the now. Hunter-gatherers didn't have to worry about meetings, traffic jams, or expensive home renovations. The struggle for survival was tough, but simple.

Once humans began settling in permanent communities, life became more comfortable but also more complex. There was greater security, but because our minds no longer had to focus solely on survival, we started dwelling on the past and worrying about the future. We began to overthink things—and we still do. How many people lie awake at night, replaying situations they think they could have handled better? How often do doubts about a new challenge keep you from sleeping?

In today's world of comfort and luxury, it has become increasingly difficult to be fully present in the moment—to completely immerse yourself in what you're doing and let go of all other concerns. Yet, that deep focus on the present is precisely what we call flow. It is a heightened state of consciousness in which we perform at our best.

Of course, it's not healthy to live without any comfort or to suffer constant hardship—that is absolutely not what I'm advocating. A series of negative experiences can break you mentally. But the sheltered life that many people now lead isn't ideal either. Balance is key. That means actively seeking out intense experiences and challenges—something many people do through sports. Especially when learning a new sport, you are fully engaged in the moment, and the feeling of flow becomes incredibly strong. Changing your daily habits or learning new skills are excellent ways to free your mind and increase your happiness.

The paradox of comfort

If modern comfort is so enjoyable, why do you still feel unhappy and unfulfilled? There are several reasons for this:

- **High expectations.** We're always comparing ourselves to others and setting higher and higher expectations. If my cousin earns that much, then I should be able to earn just as much! Social media fuels this mindset—you want to visit all those beautiful places, taste the delicious meals you see online. The seemingly perfect lives of others make you feel like you're falling short, that your own life isn't measuring up to the standard. And yet, objectively speaking, you likely live a very comfortable life. Comparing yourself to others is a shortcut to misery.
- **Lack of fulfilment.** Chasing material comfort and pleasure does not satisfy our deeper human needs. Comfort does nothing to fulfil our desire for meaning, purpose, and connection. By focusing only on comfort, we ignore what we truly need to feel good.
- **No connection with nature.** Modern comfort keeps us indoors more often and reduces our time spent in nature. And yet, natural environments have a positive effect on mental well-being. Losing our connection with nature increases stress and mental unrest. It's no surprise that some doctors are even considering prescribing nature walks to their patients.
- **Sedentary lifestyle.** Increasing automation and technological advancements are forcing more and more people into a seated existence. However, sitting for long periods is incredibly unhealthy. A lack of physical activity leads to a range of issues, including obesity and heart disease—but also mental health problems.
- **Information overload.** Through media and smartphones, we are constantly bombarded with information. It's exhausting. For your mental well-being, you need to

find a balance between media consumption and mental rest.

- **Social isolation.** Despite the internet connecting us like never before, many people feel isolated and lonely. Virtual interactions cannot fully replace real-life social contact. It's precisely those in-person experiences that we need to feel good. Sharing a meal, exchanging stories, simply being together—these moments not only bring joy but also have real health benefits.
- **Consumerism and materialism.** Our consumer-driven society and the pursuit of material wealth trap us in a vicious cycle where we constantly want more. Chasing possessions in the hope of finding happiness leads to a reality where true and lasting fulfilment remains out of reach.
- **Overstimulation and burnout.** Modern life is fast-paced and demanding. We juggle so many responsibilities that we sometimes lose track. The kids need to be dropped off at school on time, bills need to be paid, and deadlines are piling up at work. The constant stream of small and large obligations can feel overwhelming. Everyone demands a piece of your attention, overstimulating your brain. The pressure of this high-speed lifestyle can become so intense that it takes a toll on your mental health, potentially leading to burnout.
- **No more joy in simple pleasures.** The latest high-tech gadgets constantly tempt us—I own two smartwatches myself and struggle to resist them. We eagerly spend money on luxury. But this makes us less appreciative of life's small joys. An experience has to be extraordinary, top-tier—we won't settle for anything less. As a result, we overlook the happiness found in everyday moments. A bird landing on your patio table. The golden light of a sunset filtering through the leaves of a walnut tree. The

unrestrained laughter of a toddler knocking over a tower of blocks. If you no longer feel the beauty of these small moments, very little will truly move you.

- **Worries about the environment.** Our modern luxuries come at a cost—the environmental price is enormous. We are depleting natural resources, and our consumer habits generate an overwhelming amount of waste. This can leave you feeling guilty about your own consumption and travel habits. In this way, the very pursuit of comfort and extraordinary experiences can end up making you feel uneasy instead.

For the sake of clarity, I want to emphasise that the relationship between comfort and happiness is complex and varies from person to person. The points I've listed do not apply to everyone in the same way or to the same degree.

That said, there are ways to tackle the discomfort you're dealing with. Moderation and mindfulness help you rediscover the value of small moments of joy and living in the present. A holistic approach to well-being allows you to navigate the challenges of 21st-century luxury life. By making conscious choices, we can find a balance between embracing technological advancements and taking care of our mental, physical, and social well-being. That balance is essential for a happy and fulfilling life.

Radical acceptance for ultimate resilience

People don't like surprises. We crave stability and security. You probably prefer certainty over an uncertain existence, too. That's completely understandable—but unfortunately, this tendency also makes it easy to become trapped in a system. At some point, you start believing there are no other options for you. You feel stuck in your job or your company, unable to see a way out, and you resign yourself to life as it is.

The vast majority of people—98 percent of the population—are caught in this trap. They prefer not to take risks, and at the same time, they lack the curiosity and clarity to see that other possibilities exist. Or perhaps they do want to take risks, but their fear of failure is stronger than their curiosity.

Only a rare few dare to chase their dreams and embrace uncertainty. These people actively seek out discomfort because they know it will open new doors. But they don't have to be the exception—anyone can choose uncertainty. You can, too. The question is: are you willing to make that choice?

Unfortunately, the older you get, the more you become trapped by conditioning. Your upbringing, social and cultural norms, habits, and beliefs—all keep you in line. The very beliefs that bring you mental comfort also limit you, shaping both your thoughts and your actions. The hard truth is this: most of the limits we face are self-imposed. We become stuck in certain thought patterns, and as we age, change becomes increasingly difficult—both personally and professionally. We get set in our ways.

For many, this process starts immediately after graduation. They earn their degree and immediately search for a stable job. In our desire for comfort and predictability, we lock ourselves into a rigid life path.

And yet, we all have a choice. A friend once told me:

'When I graduated, I saw only one path ahead of me: get a job, find a partner, take out a mortgage. Twenty years later, I woke up. I looked back and thought: that wasn't me. That wasn't my choice—it was the choice of my family and society. But I had no other choice.'

I disagreed. 'There are so many choices you could have made!'

Many young people graduate and see a smooth, straight highway ahead of them, with clear signs pointing toward obvious destinations. Because it's the easiest route, they follow it. But they fail to notice the rough, unpaved trail between the bushes. That path doesn't reveal its destination upfront, but it's far more interesting—and opens more doors than the comfortable highway, which will never challenge you.

So: explore. Seek out new perspectives. People who chase their dreams accept uncertainty and don't shy away from discomfort.

Speaking for myself, I had no choice but to stray from the beaten path. My need for adventure was greater than my fear of uncertainty. But that uncertainty was there—and it made the adventure all the more thrilling. I have always viewed uncertainty as a tool to reinvent myself. I had no interest in shielding myself from risks and drifting into a dull, predictable life.

When I graduated from university, I could have chosen comfort. I could have opted for security—a stable job, a steady salary, and everything that comes with it. But I took a different path. Looking back, I see that I have been seeking discomfort and uncertainty my entire life. Apparently, I've always found comfort boring.

I should note that my parents gave me the freedom to choose—they never forced me into anything, allowing me to spread my own wings. They sometimes raised an eyebrow at the things I pursued. I come from a fairly traditional family, after all. My parents were both entrepreneurs—not adventurers, but they had to learn to live with uncertainty. As a business owner, you have to take risks, and I just took it a step further.

Base jumping is the most obvious example, but I take risks in everything I do. Embracing discomfort is still my way of discovering and developing myself. How far can I push myself? How can I make the best use of my skills and talents?

My discomfort zone is my personal laboratory. This is where I first test my ideas about peak performance. What works in an extreme environment, under challenging conditions, I also apply to more everyday situations. That way, I can help others by passing on my experiences.

That is exactly what I am doing with this book. Writing a book is, in itself, outside my comfort zone, but it is the perfect way to take you inside my laboratory.

I realised early on that I am more creative and productive in moments of discomfort. I react faster to my surroundings, my cognitive functions switch to turbo mode, and I feel happier and more fulfilled. For me, the essence of enjoyment is feeling myself grow and move forward. When your self-confidence grows every day, you feel grounded and strong. You, not your environment, are in control of your life.

Everyone has that choice. Do you want certainty? That's fine, but understand that it is the fastest way to give up on your dreams and follow a path that isn't truly yours. Do you want to follow your own path? Fantastic. But you will have to accept uncertainty. Acceptance is the best remedy for the restlessness that comes from an addiction to comfort.

Imagine you are faced with a difficult situation. What do you do? Do you freeze? Do you run away? Or do you stubbornly resist? These are the three classic responses, hardwired into our system: freeze, flee, or fight. But there is a fourth option: radical acceptance. You look at reality and take it as it is.

Radical acceptance means fully accepting a situation or emotion—even when it is uncomfortable or difficult. This concept, often applied in cognitive behavioural therapy, is a way to reduce mental suffering and improve emotional well-being. To practice radical acceptance, you must acknowledge and validate your feelings instead of suppressing or ignoring them. Pushing difficult emotions away only intensifies them, until they eventually overwhelm you.

Once you have acknowledged your emotions, the next step is to let go of resistance and accept reality. That does not mean you have to like a painful situation or agree with it, but it does mean you stop fighting against the fact that this is reality. Instead, you focus on finding ways to deal with it.

Radical acceptance also means you do not judge yourself for having emotions. Treat yourself with compassion and understanding. Remember that emotions are a natural part of being human. It is okay to truly feel them.

Practicing radical acceptance can be challenging. It may take time and effort before it becomes natural. But once you succeed, you will experience greater inner peace. Your well-being will improve. You will also be able to take action more effectively when a problem arises, because you will no longer waste time on endless worrying and thoughts that go in circles.

Accept things as they are. Face reality head-on. That is what radical acceptance is about. It saves you from unnecessary distress. It is a tool to manage your emotions in a healthy way and move forward in life with a more positive outlook.

Times are changing? Adapt with them

Disruptive times cause anxiety for many people. But what if you viewed times of change as opportunities for new possibilities and solutions? When certainties start to crumble, it can be difficult to focus on the positive. Here are five strategies to keep from feeling overwhelmed by unsettling news.

1. **Practice gratitude.** Take a few minutes each day to reflect on the things you are truly grateful for. This helps shift your focus from negative to positive thoughts.
2. **Reframe negative thoughts.** When you catch yourself thinking negatively, try to put a positive spin on it. If you're facing a

challenge, you might think: I'll never be able to do this. Instead, turn it into: This is a challenge, but I will find a solution!

3. **Surround yourself with positivity.** Spend time with people who have an uplifting, positive mindset. Avoid those who are constantly negative and drain your energy.
4. **Do what makes you happy.** Make time for activities that bring you joy and give you a sense of fulfilment. Not only will you naturally focus more on positive outcomes, but it will also boost your overall well-being.
5. **Practice mindfulness.** Mindfulness focuses on being present in the moment and observing your thoughts and feelings without judgement. This practice helps you become aware of negative thought patterns so that you can let them go.

Remember this: focusing on the positive is a habit that takes practice. Don't think: I can't do this. That's a negative thought. Instead, think: I'm going to give this my best effort. That is the first step toward a positive mindset. Put in the effort, give it time, and you'll see that you can train your brain to function with a much more positive outlook.

The difference between instant and delayed gratification

What gives you a sense of fulfilment? Take a moment to think about it.

Next question: what makes you happy?

One thing that certainly does not bring lasting happiness is the pursuit of instant gratification. An immediate reward does not have the same effect as a delayed reward. Unfortunately, our brain constantly pushes us to choose the immediate reward, even when it would be more rational to opt for a larger, delayed reward. This phenomenon has been well-documented in cognitive psychology, and only when you understand this mechanism do you stand a chance of resisting it.

Why does our brain deceive us this way? Neuroscientists observe a complex interplay of brain regions and neural networks that together determine how we motivate ourselves and when we feel sufficiently rewarded. One key brain region involved in resisting instant gratification is the prefrontal cortex. This area is responsible for functions such as planning, self-control, and decision-making. It plays a crucial role in regulating impulsive behaviour, weighing the costs and benefits of different actions, and selecting the appropriate course based on long-term goals. However, if this region's function is disrupted in any way, it affects the decisions you make.

Another important player is the ventral striatum, which is part of the brain's reward system. This region is activated by pleasurable stimuli such as food, sex, or drugs. When you feel an immediate sense of reward after doing something enjoyable, this part of the brain is at work. It also reinforces the behaviour that led to the pleasurable stimulus, increasing the likelihood that you will repeat it in the future.

A third area worth mentioning is the amygdala, which processes emotions. The amygdala can override rational decision-making, favouring emotionally driven impulses. The insula (or insular cortex) also becomes active when we experience an immediate reward, especially when paired with a physical sensation. On top of that, the mesolimbic dopamine system releases the neurotransmitter dopamine as a form of reward. This system plays a significant role in addiction.

Not everyone is equally prone to the temptation of instant gratification. This depends in part on how these different brain regions and networks interact. For example, people who are more impulsive and struggle to delay rewards tend to have weaker prefrontal cortex function. At the same time, their ventral striatum is more active compared to individuals who can resist temptation more effectively.

Understanding how these neural mechanisms work allows you to develop strategies to avoid falling into the same traps repeatedly. You can train yourself to exert more self-control and guide yourself toward healthier behaviours. This, for example, is how you find the motivation to lace up your running shoes and push your limits instead of staying cozy on the couch. By embracing discomfort, you will grow as a person—in more ways than one.

- **Strengthen your resilience.** When we expose ourselves to discomfort, we learn to endure challenging situations—and even thrive in them. This builds resilience and better equips you to handle future adversity.
- **Expand your comfort zone.** Stepping outside your comfort zone and embracing discomfort not only helps you grow as a person—it also brings new experiences and opportunities. You gain fresh perspectives that you wouldn't have encountered otherwise. And with each new experience, your comfort zone expands a little more.
- **Boost your creativity.** Becoming comfortable with discomfort stimulates creativity. It pushes you to think outside the box and approach problems from new angles.
- **Improve your mental health.** Avoiding discomfort leads to anxiety and stress. But when you actively seek discomfort, you confront—and overcome—your fears. This boosts your confidence and ultimately makes you happier.
- **Achieve your goals.** Seeking discomfort makes it easier to reach your goals. Sometimes, you have to push yourself past a limit, beyond your comfort zone. And when you persevere, you accomplish things you never thought possible.

Leaving your comfort zone isn't always pleasant, but the rewards are significant. Not only does it bring fulfilment, but it also makes you mentally stronger. Your resilience and creativity grow, your mental well-being improves, and you finally start achieving the goals you've set for yourself.

In the end, you are the pilot of your own life. You are the CEO of the company that bears your name—you, and no one else, make the decisions. You're fully empowered.

I believe that's an important thought: I have control over who I am. I am not a victim of unfortunate circumstances—I create the right circumstances for myself.

Happiness and where to find it

Many factors contribute to our sense of fulfilment. Think of your health. Your family. Your social environment. The place where you live. Your work. Your connections. Your financial freedom. But the greatest sense of fulfilment comes from feeling that you have control over your own life. And I believe that's also what makes you happy.

Yet fulfilment is not the same as happiness. Happiness runs much deeper. Even the most intense delayed gratification cannot compare to true happiness. Fulfilment is always about something you have experienced or achieved, while happiness is more about feeling that you have a place in the world and that you are ready for the future. That's why happiness is strongly tied to the concept of empowerment. Feeling that we have control over our lives makes us happy for several reasons.

When we feel that we are steering our own lives, we experience a sense of autonomy. We feel empowered to make our own choices and decisions. This leads to an even greater sense of fulfilment. Knowing that we are in control of our lives reduces stress because we become less vulnerable to external factors. We feel less anxious, more at ease, and more confident in our ability to face challenges.

People who have control over their lives are also better at setting meaningful goals and achieving them. And that feeling of accomplishment is incredibly satisfying. That fulfilment contributes to an overall sense of happiness. When you feel in control of your life, you also interact with others with greater confidence. The consequent positive relationships and social bonds further enhance happiness. Feeling in control gives your life a sense of meaning and purpose. You actively shape your own life and make progress toward a specific goal. That sense of intrinsic motivation is deeply fulfilling—and happiness follows.

Living your life the way you want gives you an inner sense of strength. It lays the foundation for a meaningful and fulfilling existence. As long as you understand that you cannot control everything and that uncertainty must be accepted, happiness is within reach.

I hope that all my family members experience the power of empowerment. I wish it for all my friends. I think especially of those suffering from chronic illness. Some illnesses could have been prevented; others you are born with. Some have treatments, some do not. But I believe there is always a way to turn things around.

I'm not talking about praying for a disease to disappear. The real challenge, I believe, lies in how you view your illness. What changes can you make in your own life? How can you regain some control so that, through your own actions, you can keep moving forward?

Three ways to avoid the danger of comfort

1. Seek out new experiences and learn new skills.
2. Don't run from unpleasant situations or emotions. Accept them, face them head-on, and grow as a person.
3. Actively seek out discomfort and challenge yourself to strengthen your resilience and spark your creativity.

2

Clarity shows you the way

Clarity in life is the compass that directs us towards purpose, the mirror reflecting our true values, and the light illuminating the path to meaningful choices.

Everything becomes easier with clarity. Clarity is the compass that guides you toward your goals. It is the mirror that reflects your true values. It illuminates your path to meaningful choices.

Clarity begins with awareness. And by that, I don't just mean being conscious in the literal sense, but being aware of certain fundamental things—first and foremost, yourself. Self-awareness means knowing who you are, both your strengths and your weaknesses. It allows you to recognise what you still need to work on and what you can continue to develop.

From a young age, I knew who I wanted to become and what kind of life suited me. I just didn't yet know what I wanted to do or how I would spend my future. But knowing my values was the first step toward achieving clarity in my life. Clarity also means staying calm under pressure. It means setting clear goals for yourself and understanding how those goals align with your values and your identity.

The way I describe it here, clarity seems easy to grasp. But, like so much in life, it's not always easy to apply. Our brains constantly take shortcuts and operate with cognitive biases, meaning that much of the time, we live on autopilot. That's convenient—if we had to make every tiny decision with full awareness, we would go crazy. But living too much on autopilot leads to a lack of clarity and self-awareness. You lose yourself in routines and end up without a real sense of purpose.

When we have to make an important decision, our brains unconsciously rely on what we already know and what we can already do. Because of this, we carry out many actions, behaviours, and habits automatically over time. Again, in many cases, this is useful. But if you never pause to reflect on what you're doing, you risk losing clarity. Does what I'm doing still align with who I am and what I value?

Clarity means knowing what you want to achieve, why it matters to you, and how you want to make it happen. Clarity gives you focus and allows you to make informed decisions. It enables you to take purposeful action and stay true to your goals.

I'm active in a wide range of fields and do many different things, yet I have a clear sense of what I want. That is clarity. But clarity doesn't necessarily mean knowing exactly what you want to do. That's a question I get all the time: 'What do you want to do?' But I prefer to reframe it: 'Who do you want to become in your life?'

Many young people have a clear vision early on of the path they want to take or the goal they want to reach. But sometimes, their goals are so specific that if they turn out to be unattainable, they feel completely lost.

As a young guy, I didn't know exactly what I wanted to do, but I knew who I wanted to be—someone in control of his own life, doing only what truly interested him. I knew exactly how I wanted to live, what lifestyle suited me, and my goal was always to actually live that way. I had that clarity long before I even knew the term existed.

Clarity also means knowing what you don't want to do and who you don't want to be. I didn't want to be a slave to other people's expectations, and I didn't want to do things that made money but didn't interest me. But don't ask me what I want to be doing in five years—I still don't know. And there's no point in pinning yourself down to a rigid plan and shutting out other interesting possibilities in advance.

So how do you achieve clarity? It all starts with getting to know yourself as well as possible. What are your core values as a person? The better you know yourself, the better the choices you make—and the better the results you achieve.

The way I describe it now, it might sound easy, but unfortunately, it's not. Or at least, not always. Fortunately, by now, I've already explained that a little discomfort can actually be liberating. If you only do what is expected of you and never leave your comfort zone, you will never reach clarity. People who live that way don't truly know what they're capable of or who they really are.

That is the choice you have to make: follow your own path, or follow the path set by others. Don't fool yourself—if you think you've achieved clarity without ever stepping out of your comfort zone, you might be in for a surprise. I often hear from people who spent 30 or 40 years drifting through life only to suddenly realise they didn't really know who they were or what they truly wanted. That means you've wasted half a lifetime.

That's why, for me, clarity begins with self-knowledge. I wanted to clearly understand my life goals and core values. What was my purpose, my direction? Clarity is about finding your North Star—a fixed point to guide you.

The second step is daring to ask yourself the right questions. Sometimes, this requires deep introspection, and that can be confronting. Who am I? What am I good at—and what am I not? What do I truly want? The clearer you get on these answers, the easier it becomes to achieve clarity.

A clear vision of who you want to be

From the age of eight, I imagined myself travelling the world as a top athlete or adventurer. An adventurous life was my dream. That's why I sent a drawing to my hero, oceanographer Jacques Cousteau. I saw myself as a diver aboard his legendary ship, Calypso. In my drawing, I included sharks because I was fascinated by them. To my great joy, I actually received a letter back from L'Institut Océanographique de Monaco, along with a signed photo of Cousteau.

Another possibility was becoming a pilot—I was equally fascinated by flying. I floated between the sea and the sky, and in the end, I chose the sky. But I'm still in love with the ocean, which is why I live near the coast. I didn't know exactly what I would do, but from a young age, I had a clear vision of the kind of life I wanted to lead.

For example, I never dreamed of being an accountant. Now, many accountants might say, 'Neither did I!' Yet, I often meet passionate accountants—people who are incredibly creative with numbers and love making life easier for entrepreneurs. Their fulfilment comes from the intellectual challenge. For these people, being an accountant was never the goal. Their purpose was removing obstacles and helping businesses thrive.

For me, lifestyle has always been the most important thing. I was never a career-driven person, even though my career turned out quite well in the end. My way of life always came first. The people around me, however, pursued careers and did what was expected of them. But it didn't make them happy. If they had gained clarity earlier, they might have avoided that mistake.

I recently read a biographical article about Jean-Claude Van Damme. He, too, had a crystal-clear vision of what he wanted. As a French-speaking guy from Brussels, he spoke English with a terrible accent, which made his chances of making it in Hollywood seem impossible from the start. No one ever told him, 'You have what it takes, you'll make it.' And yet, he did. He succeeded because his vision of who he wanted to be was so strong that he was determined to make his dream a reality. His goal was to have his name on the billboards of Hollywood Boulevard—and that's exactly where he ended up.

There is great strength in having a clear understanding of your goals, purpose and what drives you

Many young people lack this clarity. I meet plenty of young people who know exactly what job they want in the future, but they have no idea who they want to be or how they want to live. For me, it was the opposite: I had no idea what profession I would pursue, but I had a realistic vision of the person I wanted to become.

I am a strong believer in the Japanese concept of ikigai, which is about finding the perfect balance—doing something you love, something you're good at, and something that can support you financially. To reach that state of ikigai, you need clarity. You need to understand what you're capable of and what you need to be happy. Only then can you ask yourself: How do I turn this into a living?

Why clarity is important for success

Clarity provides a solid foundation for success

I see clarity as a beacon that illuminates the path to achievement. When uncertainty and doubt threaten to overwhelm you, clarity offers stability. It clears away the fog and confusion in your mind, turning obstacles into opportunities. Clarity is the foundation of a successful life. I see seven ways in which clarity helps you take control of your life.

1 Providing direction

Don't try to save the world. What the world needs, are people with a sense of purpose. So save yourself

You can only achieve clarity by asking yourself the right questions. What drives me? What gives me energy? What makes me happy?

Clarity starts with you, not with the outside world. It helps you identify your passions, strengths, and values. It allows you to align your goals with your true ambitions. Clarity gives you a sense of purpose, guiding your actions and decisions toward meaningful outcomes.

2 Setting goals

With clarity, you can set goals that meet the SMART criteria: Specific, Measurable, Achievable, Relevant, and Time-bound. Goals that don't meet these standards are either unattainable or meaningless.

When you have a clear vision of where you want to go, you can create a step-by-step plan. Break your journey toward a bigger goal into small, manageable steps. This makes your path realistic and achievable. That's what I've always done myself. I knew the direction I wanted to go, so every day, I took small steps toward it. This approach keeps you adaptable and allows you to adjust quickly. I never followed a straight line—when things got difficult, I took a detour. Sometimes I even took a step back and chose a new direction. The more you focus on small steps, the easier it is to shift course while still maintaining forward momentum.

Some people set a very specific goal, but it's far beyond their reach. This only creates unnecessary pressure. When your goal seems to remain out of reach, you're more likely to give up because it feels pointless. An unattainable goal doesn't motivate—it discourages. That's why it's important to keep your journey manageable. Break a big goal down into micro-goals.

This sounds simple, but it goes against human nature. Many people want control over the future. They want to reach their end goal as quickly as possible because they believe that only when they get there will they be happy. Unfortunately, that final destination is often far away. That's why it's better to focus first on controlling the present—this is how you create the future you want. The more clarity you have about the present, the more you can trust in the future.

Clarity brings peace of mind. You grow through the process, step by step, moving toward your micro-goals. Instead of stressing over distant, seemingly unreachable objectives, you stay grounded in the present moment.

3 Making decisions

The more clarity you have, the better your decisions will be—and the more those decisions will align with your vision and values. Clarity helps you evaluate choices and set the right priorities, allowing you to avoid distractions and unnecessary detours.

Making the right decision at the right time comes down to asking yourself: Does this align with what I want? To avoid mistakes, you need a strong sense of clarity—you need to know exactly what you want.

4 Focus and motivation

Clarity fuels your motivation, allowing you to stay focused and persistent in the face of challenges and setbacks

When you have clarity, you know what you're working toward and why it matters to you. This keeps you motivated and focused, even when things don't go smoothly. Clarity makes difficult or uncomfortable situations more bearable—you understand why you're doing something. The process isn't always enjoyable, but when you have a clear goal in mind, the less pleasant moments become easier to handle. Your energy is directed with precision toward the goals you're striving for.

Writing a book, for example, isn't easy or enjoyable—I won't pretend otherwise—but the end goal of creating a clear and inspiring book makes the entire process worthwhile.

5 Consistency

Clarity ensures that your actions, behaviours and choices align with your goals and values

Clarity helps you stay consistent and true to your values. Knowing exactly who you want to be prevents you from making choices that undermine your integrity or endanger your goals. Clarity is crucial for remaining credible, trustworthy, and deserving of confidence. These qualities contribute to long-term success.

6 Confidence

Knowing what you want and having a clear plan boost your confidence

Clarity helps you believe in your abilities, strengths, and potential. It builds a positive mindset that pushes you forward. I have always believed in myself, and because of clarity, I knew exactly what I was capable of—and what I wasn't. That is an enormous confidence boost.

It doesn't mean the sky is suddenly the limit, but it does provide extra fuel. If you don't know what you're capable of or where you want to go, you won't use your potential to its fullest.

And that can be demotivating. Clarity allows you to maximise your strengths—doing what you excel at gives you wings.

7 Resilience and Adaptability

Clarity doesn't mean having all the answers—not even close. But it does mean knowing what direction you want to go and how to adjust along the way when unexpected circumstances arise. It allows you to navigate obstacles, refine your strategy, and bounce back from setbacks.

Clarity gives you the strength to weather tough storms. Because you understand what you are striving for, you remain grounded, leaving little room for doubt. It also enables you to adjust your course as needed. Sometimes you need to find a way around obstacles or change tactics, but even when things go wrong, you still know exactly where you want to end up.

At its core, clarity is about a deep understanding of who you are and where you want to go. It goes beyond pure rational thought—it connects with instinct or intuition. It's about understanding through feeling, if you will. That may sound vague or abstract, but when you truly feel that you understand yourself, it creates an unmistakable, crystal-clear sensation: suddenly, you know who you are and where you are headed.

Because clarity offers so many benefits, it serves as a cornerstone of peak performance. It starts with defining your goals clearly and making the right choices. Along the way, you remain focused and consistent. Since your actions align with who you are, you can pursue your goals with confidence and perseverance. That's how success is achieved.

The golden thread in your life

Clarity makes me stronger in life. Because I have clarity in my mind, I see everything I do as part of a greater whole. I create podcasts, give keynote speeches, write books, run businesses, and fly. These may seem like completely different activities, but they are all connected. They all challenge me and carry an element of risk—both physically and emotionally. But more importantly, they share a greater purpose, a unifying story. That purpose is: to inspire myself and others.

Challenging myself inspires me, and in doing so, I can inspire others to find more fulfilment in their own lives. In my sport, I take physical risks, but because of the clarity in my mind, I am able to make the right decisions—decisions that are often a matter of life or death. To do this, I must be deeply connected to myself, without allowing my emotions, distractions, or ego to cloud my judgement. Without clarity, I could make the wrong decision—and that could be the end.

The same process applies to any career or endeavour. If you let your ego blind you, your clarity fades, and you start making poor decisions. In that case, failure can feel like a small death. That's why I work intentionally and deliberately to maintain mental clarity. With a clear head space, I don't let emotions control me.

The opposite of clarity is self-deception. A lack of clarity distances you from reality. When your ego blinds you, accidents happen. I've seen it firsthand in my sport—people who lost their clarity and paid the ultimate price. The urge to prove yourself can be literally deadly in my world.

Some people start projects with strong clarity but lose it along the way. Take the dramatic rise and fall of the Belgian tech company Lernout & Hauspie. Arrogance blinded its leaders until their collapse became inevitable. In the U.S., there was WeWork, the subject of the series WeCrashed, starring Jared Leto and Anne

Hathaway. Adam Neumann had been an unsuccessful salesman of various products until his wife told him: 'You need to find something with a clear purpose.' That's when he came up with the idea of revolutionising the shared office market. His purpose was: build a community. And for a while, it seemed to work—the company was once valued at several billion dollars. But then Neumann lost his way. He started showing up to meetings barefoot and presenting himself as a modern-day Jesus Christ. Unfortunately, he never found his holy grail. WeWork collapsed, and his dream shattered. So always stay grounded and level-headed—this is how you maintain clarity.

When you find clarity, it feels like a golden thread running through your life, holding everything together. Clarity guides you forward, leading you along unknown paths toward your deepest dreams.

May clarity be your guiding light, illuminating the path toward greatness with unwavering brilliance and grace

Tools and exercises to cultivate more clarity in your life

Once you have clarity, it becomes a powerful weapon—but how do you get that clarity in the first place? There are strategies for this. By using specific tools and exercises, you can nourish and strengthen your clarity, giving yourself the power to break through limits and unlock your full potential.

- **Define your goal with precision.** Your journey toward clarity begins with a deep dive into the core of your being.

What is the essence of who you are? What drives you? What ignites the passion in your heart? Describe your ultimate goal in such precise terms that it encapsulates the very core of your identity.

- **Master the art of prioritisation.** Not all tasks are created equal. Some open doors to success, while others are merely distractions. By setting clear priorities, you identify the actions that propel you forward and focus your energy efficiently.
- **Embrace mindfulness.** Modern life is a web of distractions. With so much coming at us, it's easy to feel overwhelmed and anxious. Fortunately, mindfulness offers an escape. It cultivates a deep sense of presence in the now, helping you become fully aware of the moment. Through mindfulness, meditation, or breathing exercises, you sharpen your clarity. Take an occasional intentional pause—a day off dedicated solely to relaxing and reflecting on yourself. Stepping away from daily routines gives you the mental space you need to gain clarity about your current situation, your aspirations, and the steps required for personal growth.
- **Cultivate creativity and inspiration.** Clarity often emerges from moments of uninhibited creativity. Even without a specific goal, creative activities are productive because they do something to your mind. Make time to express your creativity—whether through writing, painting, or simply daydreaming while immersed in nature. When you allow creativity to flow freely, clarity often follows.
- **Stay flexible and adapt.** Clarity gives you direction, but it shouldn't be treated as an iron law. Stay adaptable and adjust when circumstances change. Life is a journey filled with unforeseen obstacles. Adjust your course when necessary to avoid crashing—while still remaining true to your core values and goals.

These strategies help you maintain or strengthen your clarity. In addition, there are specific exercises that allow you to consciously create a sense of clarity.

- **Clarify your values.** Identify and rank your core values, for example, using a values wheel or ambition web. These introspective exercises help you understand what truly matters to you. As a result, you'll make decisions that lead you toward a life aligned with your beliefs.
- **30-day challenge.** Is there an activity you're currently dedicating a lot of time to, such as working out or learning a new skill? Challenge yourself to a 30-day commitment—for example, striving to reach a specific goal every day for a month. It's an intense but relatively short-term exercise that allows you to experiment and gain insights into your preferences. By the end, you'll feel a sense of accomplishment, which in turn helps you gain clarity about your aspirations.
- **Digital detox.** Put your digital devices and social media on ice for a while—(not literally, I don't want to be responsible for damaged electronics!). This intentional break frees you from mental clutter, allowing you to reconnect with your deeper thoughts. Without distractions, it becomes much easier to gain clear insight into what you truly value in life.
- **Visualise.** Imagine your ideal life in vivid detail. How do you picture the life you want to lead? Visualisation is a powerful technique that helps you sharpen your focus on what motivates you and what you are striving toward. It creates a mental blueprint of the future you want to build.
- **Decision matrix.** Create a structured framework for making important decisions by listing the pros and cons of each option. This method helps you evaluate choices objectively, showing you how each possibility aligns—or doesn't align—with your values and priorities. It's another

effective way to bring clarity to your decision-making process.

- **Seek feedback.** Find wisdom in the advice of others. Ask friends, family, or mentors for feedback on your strengths and areas for growth. These outside perspectives provide valuable insights and often lead to new clarity. None of us navigate life alone—we're all on this journey together. That's why it's smart to ask others about their experiences and how they handled them. Engage in dialogue, seek constructive feedback, and expand your perspective.
- **Practice gratitude.** Regularly express gratitude for the positive aspects of your life. Focusing on what you're thankful for cultivates a positive mindset. It reinforces your values and priorities, helping you gain clarity about what truly matters to you.

In addition to these exercises, there are various tools that can help you gain clarity. Some of these tools also support you in maintaining your exercises or committing to them for longer periods.

- **A journal.** Regularly write down your thoughts, feelings, and experiences. This technique—known as journaling—is a reflective practice that helps you explore your inner world and gain clarity about your values, goals, and concerns.
- **Mindfulness apps.** Mindfulness and meditation increase self-awareness. Apps like Headspace and Calm assist with self-reflection by offering guided sessions to help you relax and focus. By practicing mindfulness, you reconnect with your thoughts and emotions, making it easier to gain clarity when making decisions.
- **Goal-setting apps.** Apps like Trello and Todoist help you organise your goals and tasks. Breaking down a major objective into manageable steps allows you to get more

done. These apps enable you to create a structured plan, ensuring that you achieve your goals. They bring clarity to your priorities and progress.

- **The Wheel of Life.** The Wheel of Life helps you evaluate different important aspects of your life—such as your career, relationships, and health. The Wheel of Life is a visual tool used in personal development to assess balance across key life areas, such as career, health, relationships, personal growth, and more. It is typically represented as a circle divided into segments, each representing an area of life. You rate your satisfaction in each segment on a scale (e.g., 1–10), creating a 'wheel.' An uneven wheel highlights areas needing attention for a more balanced, fulfilling life. The visual representation helps you assess whether you have the right balance and whether you are finding fulfilment in your activities. This way, you can better determine where to direct your focus to achieve greater clarity and satisfaction.
- **Discover your strengths.** Tools like StrengthsFinder or VIA Character Strengths help you identify your strengths and values. Understanding these aspects forms a solid foundation for making decisions that align with your qualities, which in turn contributes to a clearer sense of purpose.

3

Accountability: a catalyst for transformation

The moment you accept total responsibility for everything in your life is the day you claim the power to change anything in your life.

Many people try to shift responsibility—whether it's toward society, their family, or their work. It feels easier, but it prevents progress. If you refuse to take responsibility, you will never truly evolve, grow, or change.

Taking responsibility and acknowledging that you may have been wrong is, in my view, a sign of intelligence. Only then can you transform. However, many people instinctively retreat into a victim mindset, believing that all their problems are caused by others. This is a dangerous way of thinking. If you see yourself as a perpetual victim, life will pass you by without you ever taking control. You start thinking: I never get lucky. Why does this always happen to me?

The opposite of taking responsibility is entitlement—believing that you deserve something, that the world owes you. This path only leads to frustration. You don't get what you want, so you start complaining. But instead, you could ask yourself: Do I actually deserve this? What have I done to earn it? If you don't take responsibility and refuse to be accountable, then I would argue that no one owes you anything.

Sometimes, the only way forward is to change the way you see things. Let me put it even more strongly: sometimes, you need to look at your entire environment from a new perspective. This exercise is known in psychology as cognitive reframing. It's a way to break free from ingrained habits. By doing this, you can escape the cycle of instant gratification and move toward true fulfilment—or even happiness. When you take responsibility and acknowledge that you haven't always handled things well, you regain control over your own life. That is what accountability is about.

Accountability isn't just a virtue—it's the cornerstone of personal growth and development. It's the catalyst for positive transformation, a foundation for progress. At its core, accountability means taking responsibility for your actions and decisions. It requires acknowledging that you play a role in shaping your life's direction. You are responsible for the consequences of your choices, habits, and actions. When you embrace this responsibility, you place yourself in a position of empowerment. You recognise that you have the ability to influence your own situation. This realisation marks the beginning of transformation. From this moment on, you are the one holding the reins. You step back into the driver's seat instead of being a passive passenger.

This sense of control—that is what truly brings fulfilment. It goes far beyond fleeting pleasures. Control gives you the sense that you are no longer just being tossed around by circumstances—you determine the course of your own life. You shape your world, you choose your direction.

For clarity's sake, let me repeat: you will never have control over everything. But people who are happy control what they can control.

When you take responsibility, you naturally engage in self-reflection and introspection. This internal process helps you recognise areas where you can improve and learn from your mistakes. It also enables you to set clearer goals and actually achieve them. In this way, accountability helps you develop your character, skills, and abilities.

Viewing mistakes as learning opportunities is an essential part of accountability. Instead of ignoring or denying your mistakes, you use them as stepping stones for self-improvement. This, in turn, strengthens your resilience and adaptability.

Thanks to accountability, you remain integrity—both toward yourself and in your relationships with others. When you honour your commitments and take responsibility for your actions, you build trust. This strengthens your foundation to become the person you want to be and to lead a life you can stand behind. That same trust also forms the basis for positive relationships, both in personal and professional contexts.

There are two ways to react when something doesn't go as planned. First, you can complain and whine. But that actually takes a lot of energy—more than you might realise. Complaining drains you emotionally and mentally, and it gets you nowhere. The second option is letting go. If something is beyond your control, there's no point wasting time or energy on it. Let it go. Instead, focus on what is within your control. This requires taking responsibility and facing your mistakes.

Let me connect this to my sport. Within my team, I expect everyone to take responsibility when something goes wrong. Did you make a mistake? Own up to it. Making mistakes is human—having the courage to admit them is superhuman. Acknowledging your mistakes is a sign of reliability that strengthens the team.

Many people struggle to own up to their failures, often because of ego. We're terrified of losing face. As social beings, we fear that admitting a mistake will cost us our status within the group. That fear runs deep—when people were exiled from their tribe in prehistoric times, they suddenly found themselves alone in the world. That's why social standing matters so much to us, and why we try to avoid losing face at all costs.

But in reality, the opposite happens when you openly admit a mistake—you actually demonstrate reliability and mental strength. Someone who bends over backwards to make excuses or shift blame onto others appears weak and untrustworthy—a liability.

Something similar happens with fear. I am not afraid to say that I feel fear, whereas many people try to deny or downplay theirs. I acknowledge my fear—and I do my best to turn it into something positive. Have I prepared properly? Have I overlooked anything? If my final checks are solid, I can trust in a good outcome. Many people, however, refuse to acknowledge their fear. They suppress it, and that is precisely what leads them to make mistakes—sometimes with fatal consequences.

Saying no is also a form of taking responsibility. In my sport, that one word can mean the difference between life and death. If I feel I'm not properly prepared or lack certain skills, I say: I'm not ready for this. I'll come back later, with better skills and better preparation. Do you see how self-awareness and responsibility go hand in hand? With clarity, taking responsibility becomes easier.

In a team, it's crucial that everyone takes responsibility instead of blaming the wind or a teammate. Owning up to mistakes is incredibly liberating—and it also shows leadership. Take responsibility for your actions, your decisions, and their consequences—because that is the first step in becoming a better, stronger version of yourself.

Cognitive reframing changes your world

The first step toward accountability is understanding: 'It's not what happened, it's how you reframe it.' The real issue isn't what happened, but how you respond to it. Consciously shifting your perspective is known as cognitive reframing. This technique—also called cognitive restructuring—is gaining traction in psychology and mental well-being. It's a tool that empowers people to approach life's challenges with a positive mindset.

Cognitive reframing originates from cognitive behavioural therapy (CBT), a widely used treatment that emphasises the connection between thoughts, feelings, and behaviour. Through cognitive reframing, you learn to recognise negative thought patterns so that you can address them. These negative thoughts often lead to stress, anxiety, and other psychological issues. By breaking these patterns, you cultivate a more optimistic and constructive outlook.

At its core, cognitive reframing means making a conscious effort to interpret or frame situations differently—seeing them in a more positive light. As a result, your emotional response to them also changes, as does your behaviour. To be clear, cognitive reframing is not about denying reality. Instead, it's about adopting a more constructive mindset that allows you to adapt more effectively to reality.

Various cognitive biases—essentially mental shortcuts or distortions—already influence how we process information. These biases shape how we perceive reality and how we respond to it. The cognitive reframing mechanism can help correct an overly negative perspective, allowing you to interpret situations in a more balanced and rational way.

One commonly used technique is the ABC Model, which stands for Activating Event, Beliefs, and Consequences. This model assumes that events trigger beliefs, which in turn influence our emotions and behaviour. By changing negative beliefs, you can also change how you react to them.

Besides a positive mindset, cognitive reframing has three major benefits:

1. **Less stress.** Cognitive reframing allows you to see a challenging situation differently, which means you also respond differently. This reduces the physical and psychological impact of events that would normally cause stress. If you've been struggling with stress for a long time, cognitive reframing is the way to break the vicious cycle.
2. **Better problem-solving.** A positive mindset boosts your creativity and improves your ability to solve problems. When you view challenges as opportunities, you become better at actually finding solutions. Thanks to cognitive reframing, you no longer allow yourself to be paralysed by difficulties.
3. **Greater emotional well-being.** Cognitive reframing strengthens your emotional resilience and helps you manage negative emotions. A positive outlook contributes

to both your mental well-being and overall psychological health.

By actively working on cognitive reframing, you break free from limiting thought patterns and cultivate a more optimistic perspective on the challenges that come your way. Is there a problem? Great—either you solve it, or you adapt.

Like any other skill, cognitive reframing requires practice and consistency. But the long-term benefits make it well worth the effort. Take it from me: if you put in the work to master cognitive reframing, you'll be far happier in the long run than if you choose the resentful path of entitlement.

The pitfall of entitlement

Do you believe that someone owes you something? That you're entitled to something, for whatever reason? Then let me hit you with a hard truth: no one owes you anything. You are not entitled to anything.

Some people think: The government owes me a job. Or: My employer owes me a raise. And job security. And a comfortable work environment. Entrepreneurs say: My business deserves subsidies, and taxes should be lower. There are single men who think they deserve a woman. Some women believe it's normal for their partner to always pick up the check at a restaurant. And plenty of adult children expect free housing at Hotel Mama for years on end.

Time and again, it all comes down to the same thing: entitlement—the idea that 'They owe me...' Well, sorry, but they owe you nothing. Just because you expect something doesn't mean you have a right to it. And even if you do have a legal right to something, you should still ask yourself: What can I do? How can I improve myself?

Because if you just sit around waiting and don't take action, you lose control over your own life—and you turn yourself into a victim.

I fully support people taking care of their mental health. But I also think it's unhealthy to assume that your employer is solely responsible for it. Some people become so fixated on the concept of mental health that they lose their resilience and adaptability. They shift all responsibility onto their employer or their environment and stop taking initiative themselves.

My motto is: take care of yourself. You are responsible for your mental health. You decide how much workload you can handle.

A lot of employees stay late at the office to prove how dedicated they are, hoping it will earn them a raise or a promotion. But what they actually earn is exhaustion and burnout.

You need to take responsibility for going home on time, for taking care of your children, or for whatever else matters in your life. Sitting behind your computer longer without actually doing more accomplishes nothing.

People who lack responsibility and have too much entitlement are dependent. Essentially, they are no longer capable of taking care of themselves. And if you can't take care of yourself, you let your entire team down.

When I lead a team, I always prepare thoroughly. But at the start, I also make it clear: 'Everyone is responsible for their own actions. Your mental health is in your own hands. Dare to say 'no' and be honest about your mistakes.'

That mindset is just as important when raising children. Teach them that they can't just expect everything to be handed to them—that they, too, must take responsibility. That way, they grow up to be independent citizens. Easier said than done? I know from personal experience that it's not always so straightforward. My own son, for example, often tries to shift blame onto someone else. If he forgets his school planner, suddenly it's someone else's fault, and he thinks it's unfair that the teacher calls him out on it. But it was his responsibility to bring his planner—he can't expect someone else to do it for him. Like many people, he sometimes acts as if 'It's not my fault—it's the universe's fault!'

So I tell him: 'The day you take responsibility for yourself is the day you truly become an adult.' He laughs about it now, but soon enough, he'll realise that's just how life works.

When I pack my parachute for a jump and something goes wrong, that's my responsibility. When I make a mistake as a helicopter pilot, I can't just blame others—I made that mistake, and no one wronged me. A commercial airline captain, for example, is responsible for their passengers and must ensure their team functions properly. That's what we call airmanship.

In 'Doe, dump of delegeer' (LannooCampus, 2024), author Rik Moons—who specialises in leadership and is also a flight instructor—shares an insightful anecdote about entitlement.

One day, there was a strong crosswind—a side wind that makes takeoff and landing much more difficult. Moons advised a fellow pilot against flying, but the pilot insisted and even asked Moons to accompany him. When Moons declined, the pilot took off anyway. During the landing, the crosswind got the better of him: his plane veered off the runway, causing significant damage. But instead of admitting his mistake, the pilot blamed Moons:

'See? This wouldn't have happened if you had flown with me!'

The audacity—to pin all the blame on the colleague who had actually taken responsibility by warning him about the risk. You see the same thing all the time in news reports about drunk driving checkpoints:

'But officer, I wasn't driving far!'

'I was the only one who knew the way home!'

'My wife has night blindness!'

The excuses from these so-called 'victims' are endless, and the police officers stopping them are suddenly framed as villains, unfairly ruining their night out. A friend of mine, who is a police officer, has heard every excuse in the book—nothing surprises her anymore. The only thing that would still shock her is if someone immediately admitted:

'Officer, you're absolutely right. I drank too much, and I have no excuse for it. Here are my keys. I'll call a taxi and pay my fine.'

What police officers hear all the time: 'Don't You Have Anything Better to Do?'

The entitlement and lack of responsibility behind that question are truly mind-boggling. My friend responds to it with: 'No, we don't have anything better to do, because people die on the road every day.'

I was once pulled over for speeding myself. The officers were surprised that I immediately admitted my mistake and didn't argue.

Teachers and professors constantly hear excuses when students fail to complete their assignments. The dog ate my homework. My computer crashed. There was a death in the family. Every excuse seems good enough to avoid taking responsibility. But no—just say: 'My apologies, I forgot.'

The discussion about obesity is a sensitive topic. I don't want to point fingers at people with obesity because the food industry is notorious for its deceptive practices, and many advertisements for so-called healthy products are misleading.

At the same time, some people with obesity claim they cannot do anything about it. Their hormones, their genetics, their environment—it's all working against them. They genuinely believe they're doing everything possible to lose weight. But when you actually look at how many calories they consume versus how many they burn, you can see that their story doesn't entirely add up—that they could be making more of an effort. Unfortunately, this goes against human nature. Taking responsibility and making an effort? Pff, that's too hard. People prefer to believe they deserve a magic pill that will make them lose weight effortlessly.

Obesity is often influenced by psychological issue—people have been made addicted to fatty and sugary foods. In addition to the marketing strategies of food producers and supermarkets, our eating culture plays a role. That's all true. But nothing is stopping you from seeking help and getting guidance. Nothing—except your own willingness to take responsibility. It's harsh to say, but the information about a healthy diet is out there. If you ignore it or refuse any form of professional help, then it is your own responsibility when you continue to carry those extra pounds. Cutting back on processed foods, alcohol, and inactivity already makes a massive difference. And yet, many people only take action when their body finally sounds the alarm—and by then, it's often too late. Are these people victims? Yes—but not only of the food industry. They're also victims of their own lack of self-awareness and discipline. They chase instant gratification and comfort.

Why am I saying this so bluntly? To make the message clear: YOU hold the reins. YOU have the power to turn your life around. Stop seeing yourself as a victim. Stop expecting others to save you. Take action. I'm not saying you can't ask for help or that you have to fix everything alone. What I am saying is: go find a solution. That's why I have an issue with the normalisation of obesity. Of course, I don't want people with obesity to be excluded from society, and I understand that they're tired of being shamed. That's neither pleasant nor fair. But at the same time, obesity is, in most cases, the result of an unhealthy lifestyle. When you normalise obesity under the banner of body positivity, you're essentially saying that an unhealthy lifestyle is okay. It's not okay. Because later in life, obesity leads to numerous conditions that drastically reduce quality of life—diabetes, cardiovascular disease, and cancer. There's also a link to anxiety disorders and depression. These illnesses don't just cause personal suffering—they also cost society enormous amounts of money.

I know someone who couldn't bear the sight of his ever-growing weight anymore. He didn't feel good in his own skin. Instead of letting himself be convinced that his obesity wasn't that bad, he took the initiative to go to his doctor, a dietitian, and a fitness coach. He realised: I need guidance because I can't do this alone. But it's still my responsibility to seek help.

It's your responsibility to age healthily. While the healthcare system and society play important roles, relying solely on them isn't always helpful. Preventing problems is always better than trying to fix them later. Many people over eighty now regret not taking better care of their health when they were younger: 'If only I had exercised more, eaten healthier, and drunk less.'

When I turn eighty, I want to be able to say: I did everything I could to stay as healthy as possible so I can enjoy my old age with a good quality of life. And yet, some people still look at me strangely when they hear I don't drink alcohol anymore: 'But everyone dies, whether you drink or not.'

Sure—everyone dies. But I want to stay healthy for as long as possible. I don't want to spend the last fifteen years of my life stuck in a chair in front of the television. I want to live, fully. Many elderly people regret enjoying the good things in life a little too much. A craving was easily satisfied with something sweet or an extra portion of meat. But that craving wasn't real hunger—it was just wanting something, a form of instant gratification. That's why I find the concept of intuitive eating interesting. It's about eating consciously and intentionally. You listen to your body and decide if and how much you eat. It's the opposite of entitlement. Instead of automatically indulging every craving, you ask yourself: 'Is this truly what my body needs?' That's a completely different mindset. A mindset of accountability.

How entitlement blocks the path to success

People who believe they naturally deserve privileges or special treatment are, by definition, entitled. But that mindset is useless—in fact, entitlement can have a massive negative impact on your personal relationships, workplace atmosphere, and even society as a whole. A healthy sense of self-worth is necessary for fulfilment, but it becomes a problem when you assume you automatically deserve things. Because, in reality, entitlement often leads to the opposite of what you expect: rejection, frustration, and failure. Here's how:

- **Strained relationships.** Entitlement destroys relationships. If you always expect more than others, you'll struggle to show empathy. When you prioritise your needs and desires over those of your friends, family, or colleagues, it creates tension and jealousy. An egocentric mindset leads to conflicts, communication breakdowns, and, eventually, the collapse of meaningful connections.
- **Unrealistic expectations.** Entitled people often have completely unrealistic expectations. They believe they deserve praise or success without putting in any effort. But when those expectations inevitably go unmet, they experience constant disappointment and frustration. Over time, this leads to a deep sense of dissatisfaction—they struggle to handle setbacks and fail to adapt to changing circumstances.
- **Lack of accountability.** Entitlement and accountability are complete opposites. If you believe you deserve privileges without working for them, you're refusing to take responsibility for your own actions. Instead, you assume the world owes you something. This mindset not only stunts your personal growth but also creates friction in your environment. Entitlement goes against social fairness, equality, and civic duty.

- **Stunted professional growth.** Feeling entitled at work is a career killer. Employees who expect promotions or recognition without putting in effort often lack motivation. And when they don't get the rewards they assumed were guaranteed, they feel rejected and disengaged. This leads to poor performance, resentment, and a toxic work atmosphere—dragging down both individual success and team productivity.
- **Resistance to change.** Entitled people resist change because they see it as a threat to their 'rights.' But this resistance blocks personal development and makes them unable to adapt to new challenges or opportunities. In a world that's evolving faster than ever, that kind of attitude will leave you completely behind.

The best way to avoid entitlement in yourself? Self-awareness, empathy, and effort. By recognising that entitlement only leads to frustration, you'll find it much easier to shift to a healthier, more productive mindset.

Learning to cope with injustice

The world is full of injustice. But that doesn't mean we should blame others for our circumstances. Life is full of struggles and hardship, but that doesn't mean we have to despair. Unfortunately, there are countless examples of people who found life so cruel and unfair that they saw only one drastic solution. Take the Russian author Leo Tolstoy, for instance. He found existence in this world so absurdly unjust that he suggested there were only four possible responses: childlike ignorance, hedonistic pleasure, suicide, or struggling on despite everything. Tolstoy analyzed these four options in his essay 'A Confession', and concluded that suicide was the most honest response. Continuing to struggle, he argued, was a sign of personal weakness—an inability to react appropriately to the absurdity of life. And yet, despite this bleak outlook, Tolstoy stubbornly kept pushing forward.

Tragically, some individuals who feel overwhelmed by injustice and isolation have responded with violence, as seen in devastating incidents. Consider the many American school shootings, with Sandy Hook and Columbine being among the most infamous. The United States has seen thousands of mass shootings where perpetrators killed at least four others before taking their own lives.

Despite Tolstoy's grim worldview—and despite the fact that suffering may seem to affect you more harshly than others—blaming the world for your misfortune is pointless. You must take responsibility for yourself.

The Russian author Aleksandr Solzhenitsyn had a completely different perspective from his compatriot Tolstoy. Solzhenitsyn believed that cruelty could be rejected, even if life had been cruel to you. He spoke from experience. During World War II, he fought alongside the Communists against the Nazis, yet despite his service, he was sent to a forced labour camp after the war—for the crime of criticising dictator Joseph Stalin in private letters. As if life in the gulag weren't punishment enough, he was also diagnosed with cancer. And yet, Solzhenitsyn did not blame the world for his suffering. He accepted his fate and decided to use the time he had left to do something meaningful. He wrote 'The Gulag Archipelago', a book that was both a historical account and a condemnation of the Soviet labour camps where he had endured so much. His work played a major role in eroding intellectual support for Stalinism in certain circles.

The paralysing effects of a lack of accountability

Without accountability, there is no personal growth or development. In order to grow, you must take responsibility for your actions and their outcomes—whether they are positive or negative Without accountability, real change is impossible. But accountability is more than just admitting to mistakes or accepting praise for your successes. It goes deeper than that. It encompasses self-awareness, responsibility, and the ability to make choices that align with your values and goals. When you hold yourself accountable, you recognise that you are in control of your actions and that their consequences are also in your hands. This sense of ownership empowers you to create change and bring yourself closer to your aspirations.

Unfortunately, accountability isn't easy. Many people struggle with it in various aspects of life—whether it's their health, career, or relationships. A lack of accountability manifests in different ways:

- **Blaming others.** When you refuse to take accountability, you always attribute your problems to external factors—your upbringing, your boss, your partner, or circumstances beyond your control. This mindset allows you to shift responsibility onto others, which ultimately prevents you from improving yourself.
- **Procrastination.** Avoiding responsibility often leads to procrastination. When you don't feel accountable for your goals, you are less motivated to take action, making it easier to delay what needs to be done.
- **Stagnation.** Without accountability, you become complacent and get stuck in your comfort zone. You start believing that change is unnecessary or even impossible.
- **Repeating Mistakes.** If you fail to take responsibility for your actions and their consequences, you're more likely

to repeat your mistakes. If you don't acknowledge where you went wrong and learn from it, you simply won't grow.

- **Damaged Relationships.** A lack of accountability can harm relationships. Blaming others or refusing to take responsibility for your actions leads to conflicts and erodes trust.
- **Decreased Productivity.** In a professional setting, a lack of accountability results in lower productivity. If you don't take ownership of your tasks and ignore the results (or the lack thereof), you won't be able to excel or improve.
- **Reduced Well-Being.** Personal fulfilment and well-being are closely tied to accountability. When you hold yourself accountable, you make better choices that contribute to your physical and mental health. On the flip side, you won't feel any real satisfaction from tasks or personal projects if you don't take responsibility for them.

A lack of accountability is a major barrier to personal growth and transformation. Only by acknowledging your responsibility, facing the consequences of your actions, and actively working on self-improvement can you break free from this cycle. This is how you take major steps toward the life you truly want to lead.

How to embrace accountability

Tackling a lack of accountability is a big step toward a more fulfilling life. It's not easy, but these strategies will help you take responsibility for your actions. You'll also find that it accelerates your growth, both personally and professionally.

- **Self-Reflection** – Observe your own behaviour and try to identify areas where you avoid responsibility. Recognise the patterns and habits that are holding back your personal growth.

- **Set Clear Goals.** Define your goals and break them down into manageable steps. This allows you to create a roadmap for progress and reinforces your sense of responsibility.
- **Seek Support.** Share your goals with a trusted family member, friend, coach, or therapist. Having someone to hold you accountable while also offering guidance can make a big difference.
- **Learn from Your Mistakes.** Instead of dwelling on failures or denying them, see them as learning opportunities—chances to grow. Face your mistakes, understand why they happened, and take steps to prevent them from recurring.
- **Be Consistent.** Develop a strong sense of accountability by consistently making choices that align with your values and goals. Consistency is the key to long-term accountability and personal success.

Cognitive reframing in practice

With cognitive reframing, you're less likely to fall into the trap of entitlement and instead develop into someone who takes full responsibility for their actions and decisions. While the concept of cognitive reframing seems simple, applying it in real life can be challenging. Fortunately, there are practical steps you can take to shift your perspective and become more accountable.

- **Mindfulness and Awareness.** Practicing mindfulness teaches you to observe your thoughts without immediately judging them. When you become aware of your thinking patterns, you can identify negative thoughts and redirect them before they spiral.
- **Challenge Negative Thoughts.** Question negative thoughts by asking yourself whether they are based on

facts or just assumptions. Look for evidence that supports or contradicts your thinking, allowing you to cultivate a more objective mindset.

- **Positive Affirmations.** Try replacing negative self-talk with positive affirmations. This influences your thought processes, reinforces constructive beliefs, and helps you develop a more optimistic outlook.
- **Humour and Playfulness.** Using humour in challenging situations offers a fresh perspective and reduces emotional tension caused by negative thoughts. A playful attitude naturally fosters cognitive reframing, making you less rigid and more adaptable to life's difficulties.
- **Reinterpreting Events.** Consider viewing setbacks differently. Instead of seeing failure as a defeat, frame it as a valuable learning opportunity. This shift in perspective strengthens your resilience and emotional endurance.

4

How limiting beliefs paralyse you

*The only limits you have
are the ones
you set yourself.*

Do you ever tell yourself, 'I can't do this'? It sounds like a fact, but it's just an idea—a thought that unknowingly holds you back.

Often, the only thing stopping you from reaching your full potential is the boundaries you impose on yourself. Limiting beliefs are invisible chains that prevent you from taking important steps. These self-imposed limits develop gradually, shaped by our upbringing, social environment, culture, or religion. Breaking free from these mental barriers is essential for personal growth, success, and fulfilment. To do so, you first need to understand what limiting beliefs are, how they manifest, and what you can do to overcome them.

Limiting beliefs are negative thoughts that hinder progress and restrict your potential. They can appear in relationships, careers, personal development, and self-image. They often originate from past failures, criticism from others, or comparisons with other people's success. These beliefs take many forms, including:

- 'I don't have the experience or skills for this.'
- 'I will never be able to reach that goal.'
- 'I'm too old for this.'
- 'Now isn't the right time.'
- 'I don't deserve success.'

These may seem like rational reasons, but in reality, they are excuses we use to avoid trying. We hide behind them to avoid failure, but in doing so, we also miss valuable opportunities to grow.

More often than not, we are more afraid of failing in front of others than of actually trying something new. You've probably heard of FOMO (fear of missing out), but there's also FOPO: fear of other people's opinions.

A few years ago, I spoke at a large IT company. After my presentation, I had a long conversation with a woman who had worked as a secretary for twelve years. One day, a position opened up in sales, and she felt tempted to go for it. But instead of taking the leap, doubt crept in. 'Can I even do this?' she thought. She felt trapped in her role—she had never sold anything before. But in the end, she took the chance.

'And I became really good at it,' she told me. 'I even became the best salesperson on the entire team—after twelve years at the reception desk.'

I've heard many similar stories. So many people have talents, skills, and experiences that could easily be applied in a different role. But they either don't realise it or don't dare to try.

Surprisingly, many dentists and general practitioners suffer from burnout. 'You study for years to become a dentist,' one former dentist explained to me. 'You know you'll earn a good living. You have a financial guarantee, but what you don't know is whether it will actually make you happy.'

And that's exactly the problem—many doctors chose security, but it doesn't fulfil them. Yet, many of them genuinely believe they aren't capable of doing anything else.

That idea is completely wrong. Doctors, by definition, are intelligent people who analyze complex issues and process large amounts of information. With that skill set, they have countless career options.

'I've been a dentist for twenty years—how can I suddenly become an entrepreneur?' That was the doubt a former dentist once had. But in the end, he took the leap. One day, he simply switched careers—and succeeded. Looking back, he realised that quitting dentistry had been harder than succeeding as an entrepreneur.

I've told rugby players nearing the end of their careers the same thing: Take all your skills and talents into a new job, and you have a high chance of success. You understand discipline and work ethic. You're familiar with failure and know how to deal with setbacks. At the same time, you're used to pushing through no matter what. You already have these qualities, and they are incredibly valuable.

This is exactly why so many companies actively seek out former top athletes—their mindset matters far more than a few technical skills that can easily be taught. And yet, many elite athletes struggle with depression after their careers end. They strongly associate their sport with their personal identity. When their sport is gone, they lose their sense of self, and limiting beliefs start creeping in.

I believe we all struggle with these kinds of limiting beliefs—it's just harder for some people to break free from them. But in the end, they're always just excuses. When you say, 'I can't do this,' what you often mean is, 'I'm afraid of failing in front of others, so I'd rather not try at all.'

At that point, you have two choices. Either you accept the limitation and stay where you are, or you ask yourself: 'What's the first step I can take toward my goal?'

This is the difference between a fixed mindset and a growth mindset. A fixed mindset can develop at a very young age—unfortunately. If, as a child, you're constantly told you're bad at something, you start believing it. The same happens at work. If your boss or colleagues keep telling you, 'You're not good at communicating,' you'll internalise it over time. Limiting beliefs can come from within, but they're often imposed by the people around you. The key to breaking free is to ask yourself:

'What is holding me back from reaching my goals today? What are my mental barriers?'

Top athletes often sigh, 'I'll never reach that goal—it's too far out of my league.' Or someone confidently states, 'I can't draw.' Whenever I hear that, I ask, 'And how long have you practiced that skill to be so sure?' The usual response? 'Well, I've never actually practiced it.' I also often hear, 'I'm terrible at music. I can't sing at all.' But contrary to what many people believe, most people actually can sing—unless they're truly tone-deaf. People used to sing together more often, and in Iceland, that tradition is still going strong. But in many other cultures, a social barrier has emerged: singing is only for the stage, and if you're not on a stage, you shouldn't even try. That's a limiting belief. So no, you're not 'bad at singing'—you just haven't learned how to do it yet.

When Roger Federer and Rafael Nadal dominated tennis in the early 2000s, every competitor believed that the only way to beat them was if they had an off day and you got incredibly lucky. But then, a young Serbian player arrived on the scene and boldly declared, 'I can beat Roger and Rafa.'

The tennis world was outraged at such arrogance. But it wasn't arrogance—it was self-confidence. And he proved himself right. That young player was Novak Djokovic, and he went on to form the legendary Big Three alongside Federer and Nadal. Djokovic doesn't just have extraordinary talent—he never limited himself and always did everything in his power to go as far as possible. That mindset is what separates the absolute elite from the rest.

Make no mistake: I, too, have limiting beliefs. The first time someone asked me to speak in public, two thoughts flashed through my mind. The first: 'Help! I can't do this.' Public speaking was completely outside my comfort zone—I simply couldn't do it. Worse still, I had always been terrible at speaking in front of a class at school. As a child, I would lose sleep whenever I had to give a presentation. It became a vicious cycle: if you convince yourself that you can't do something, and your environment—your teacher, your classmates—reinforces that belief, you end up truly believing it.

But almost immediately, a second thought followed: 'Maybe I can learn to do this? And what do I have to lose?' So I asked myself: 'What's the first step to getting better at this?' I figured I might as well give it a shot—after all, despite my own limiting beliefs, others believed I could do it. That first talk went much better than expected. The result? What once seemed impossible became my new normal.

Speaking to five hundred people? Not unusual anymore. Sure, I still get nervous before a lecture, but now I know how to handle it.

The best way to counter limiting thoughts is to first become aware of them—and then take action. If I had stuck with my first thought, I would have never picked up a microphone, stepped onto a stage, or built a career as a speaker. But I took the risk, and now I'm even writing books: I dared to jump.

Instead of limiting yourself, ask: 'What first step can I take?' You don't need to aim for perfection. Simply trying something new can shift the entire direction of your career—or even your life.

When people hear that I practice base jumping, they're often impressed. 'I'd love to do that! But could I?'

My answer is always the same: 'Yes, of course!'

You'll get hurt. You'll have to learn how to manage risk and fear. You'll have to invest a huge amount of time into training. But if you truly want to do it, you can achieve it—step by step. That's the student mindset—something I've had throughout my career. It means questioning yourself (but not too much) and, above all, staying curious. The most powerful question you can ask is: 'How can I learn this?'

That question has shaped my life and expanded my potential. Without it, you'd close countless doors before they even have a chance to open. If you never ask yourself how to learn something, you trap yourself in your limiting beliefs. You turn them into excuses—excuses not to take action. We'd rather convince ourselves we can't do something than risk experiencing failure firsthand.

With AI assistants like ChatGPT on the rise, I often hear older colleagues sigh: 'I don't understand how AI works, and I'm too old to learn.'

No. You're not too old—you just don't want to learn.

Some people complain, 'I just can't keep up with the times.'

No. You don't want to keep up with the times.

A friend once told me: 'I'd love to be an entrepreneur, but that's just not possible. My whole family works in government—business isn't in our blood.'

That's nonsense! As if your family's profession somehow makes you genetically unfit to start a business. That's a perfect example of a limiting belief. I told him: 'You're just hiding behind excuses. Deep down, you know you're smart enough to do this. But you're afraid of failing, so you're looking for a way out before you even try.'

There are always ways to learn something new. If your desire and motivation are strong enough, you'll find a way. Unless you're the one standing in your own way.

I once had a conversation with a sales team manager who brought up a very specific issue: when salespeople saw that a potential customer was already working with a competitor, they gave up immediately. They thought, 'Why bother? They already have someone.' But instead, they should have been asking, 'Maybe they're not happy—what if we can offer them something better?' Sure, they might still say no, but so what? Out of fear of hearing 'no,' many people don't even try for a 'yes' and settle for rejection before it even happens. Do you see the problem? You're afraid of hearing 'no,' so you choose 'no' for yourself.

If you pay attention, you'll notice limiting beliefs everywhere. People who dream of opening a restaurant crush their own ambitions with, 'Oh, but there are already so many restaurants.' Sure, but maybe you have a fresh concept? Some young people have an incredible idea for a startup but sigh, 'I just don't have the money to make it happen.' Then go find the money! Either you're not truly convinced of your idea, or you're too scared of failure.

Now, not every self-critical thought is a limiting belief. I have cool ideas sometimes—like launching a certain product—but then I realise I don't feel like dealing with the logistics that come with it. If you love cooking but hate administration and pressure, maybe opening a restaurant isn't the right move. A limiting belief is something you genuinely want to do but don't dare to pursue. The key is making conscious choices. If you're missing a skill—learn it. But don't dive into ventures that don't align with your values and interests. You don't have to say yes to everything—know yourself and what suits you.

The impact of limiting beliefs

Limiting beliefs can affect every area of your life.

- **Stalled personal growth.** Limiting beliefs create a fixed mindset, where you cling to what you already have and know, without growing. With this mindset, you avoid challenges and stop learning from mistakes. Both personally and professionally, you stop progressing. Fear of failure plays a big role here. Ironically, it's that same fear that makes you miss out on success that was actually within your reach.
- **Shaky self-confidence.** Limiting beliefs chip away at your self-confidence, making it harder to seize opportunities, speak up, and take risks. Fear of failure is constantly lurking over your shoulder. You convince yourself you're not smart enough for a certain job, or not attractive enough for someone you're interested in. You'd rather reject yourself than risk being rejected by someone else. It saves face in the moment, but ultimately, it erodes your self-esteem.
- **Strained relationships.** Limiting beliefs shape how we see ourselves in relation to others, leading to insecurities and jealousy. This makes it harder to build or maintain meaningful relationships. Someone who believes they're unworthy of love often sabotages their relationships—if

only to prove themselves right: 'See? I knew I wasn't good enough.'

Limiting beliefs hold you back in so many ways. If you truly convince yourself of a limitation, it becomes a self-fulfilling prophecy. Because you don't believe in your own success, you subconsciously sabotage your efforts to achieve your goal. It's as if you'd rather be right about your limiting belief than prove it wrong.

Cutting back on limiting beliefs

When I started giving lectures, I thought: I need to learn how to speak in front of people and how to structure my content. After my first talk, I realised: step one is done—now I can focus on improving. Step two was learning how to deliver a relevant, well-structured story. And so, I kept building on that. I was searching for the perfect step-by-step plan. But that perfect plan doesn't exist.

Most successful entrepreneurs had no idea what their idea or project would ultimately become. The most important step was simply getting started and staying open to learning along the way. Look at Mark Zuckerberg, the creator of Facebook. When he launched Facebook, he had no clue it would evolve into a tech giant. Until 2014, Facebook's internal motto was: 'Move fast and break things.' Just go for it and figure things out as you go.

You don't need a grand plan. What you need is the right mindset. By tinkering, experimenting, and absorbing knowledge from different sources, you improve and make progress. It's a continuous process. The student mindset never ends—there is no final destination. You've set off a chain reaction, and the only thing fueling this never-ending story is your attitude. That mindset helps push back against limiting beliefs.

Limiting beliefs are deeply ingrained in our thinking—it's not easy to shake them off. But you don't have to be stuck with them forever. The first step in overcoming limiting thoughts is to recognise and acknowledge them. Whenever you think, 'I can't do this' or 'I'm not good enough,' that's already a sign: Oops, that was a limiting thought. Consider keeping a journal to track these thoughts so you become aware of the beliefs that are holding you back. Once you see them clearly, you can challenge them.

When you notice negative thoughts, question their validity. Don't beat yourself up for having them—just ask: Is there actual evidence for this belief, or is it based on assumptions and biases?

The second step is embracing a growth mindset. That means not freezing in the face of challenges but seeing them as opportunities to learn and grow. Understand that you develop new skills by putting in the effort and immersing yourself in new experiences. A growth mindset is the key to eliminating limiting thoughts. Face challenges head-on, learn from mistakes, and surround yourself with positive influences—that's the path to self-improvement. Focus on getting better. You don't have to strive for perfection, just keep learning and growing. Seize every opportunity to expand your knowledge and develop new skills. Replace limiting beliefs with positive affirmations. That way, you reprogramme your brain and cultivate a stronger, more optimistic mindset. Instead of thinking, 'I can't do this,' tell yourself, 'I am resourceful and capable.'

A powerful tool is visualisation. Instead of focusing on failure, picture yourself achieving your goal. Visualise success and focus on the positive emotions that come with it. Another helpful strategy is seeking support. Share your thoughts and fears with someone you trust—a friend, coach, or therapist. An outside perspective can bring new insights and help challenge and eliminate limiting beliefs.

Finally, break big goals into smaller, achievable steps. Celebrating small wins builds confidence and strengthens your belief in your abilities.

All of this isn't easy—limiting beliefs are strong barriers blocking our path. They prevent us from fully realising our potential. However, the moment you recognise and challenge these beliefs, you've already taken a huge step toward personal growth and success. If you actively work on your mindset, reinforce positive affirmations, and don't hesitate to seek support, you'll be well on your way to overcoming the thoughts that hold you back. Most importantly, don't tell yourself you can't break free from limiting beliefs. No, it's not easy—but difficult does not mean impossible. It takes effort, but that effort is worth it because the reward is fulfilment and success.

Remember: your potential is limitless. Limiting beliefs serve you in no way.

Empower yourself through self-reliance

Few things contribute as much to personal growth as self-reliance—the belief that you are capable of completing tasks and achieving goals. The world-renowned Canadian psychologist Albert Bandura emphasised in the 1970s how crucial self-efficacy is in shaping our behaviour, motivation, and resilience. By strengthening our self-reliance, we unlock our potential and pave the way for success. Self-reliance is more than confidence—it's the belief that you have the ability to take the necessary actions to achieve a desired outcome. This belief is built on your past experiences, skills, and willingness to learn. People with high self-reliance tend to approach challenges with optimism and perseverance. They believe they are in control of their actions. On the other hand, low self-reliance often leads people to shy away from obstacles or give up too easily.

Studies consistently show that self-reliance is a game-changer—in personal life, professional careers, and athletic performance. Those who are self-reliant set higher goals, work harder, and persist despite setbacks. This attitude almost inevitably leads to greater success. Low self-reliance, however, limits aspirations, hinders top performance, and contributes to a sense of helplessness.

Self-reliance fuels motivation. When people believe in their ability to overcome difficulties, they see challenges as temporary hurdles rather than insurmountable barriers. This resilience allows them to bounce back from failure, learn from experiences, and keep striving towards their goals with renewed determination.

When you replace limiting beliefs with self-reliance, you're fully prepared to become who you want to be and live the life you've always dreamed of.

Five steps to strengthening self-reliance

Self-reliance is something you can develop and reinforce. If you struggle with it, you don't have to accept that as your reality—there are concrete steps you can take to improve it.

1. **Success builds confidence.** By setting achievable goals and gradually increasing the challenge, you create a series of success experiences. Each success strengthens your belief in your own abilities.
2. **Learn by example.** Watching others overcome obstacles and succeed can increase your own confidence in your ability to do the same. Role models and inspiring mentors are powerful sources of motivation.
3. **Social encouragement.** When others spur you on and give you positive feedback, it boosts your self-reliance. Being surrounded by a supportive environment fosters a growth mindset. Celebrating your efforts and progress with others reinforces your confidence and persistence.

4. **Emotional regulation.** Learning to manage your fears, doubts, and negative emotions is essential for maintaining self-reliance. Techniques like mindfulness, cognitive reframing, and stress management help you build resilience.
5. **Lifelong learning.** To grow and continue evolving, you must constantly embrace new challenges, seek feedback, and develop new skills. Every time you successfully complete a new task, your self-reliance strengthens.

The psychologist Albert Bandura saw self-reliance as a powerful source of happiness: 'People who believe they have the power to exercise control over their own lives are healthier, work more effectively, and are more successful than those who do not believe they can change their lives.' Self-reliance opens doors and turns dreams into reality.

5

Break free from rigid social norms

Living your life on your own terms requires breaking societal and culturally outdated rules.

Whenever you start something new, there's always fear: what if this fails? Sometimes, that fear stops you from taking the leap. But it's not necessarily failure itself that we fear—it's how the people around us will react. Will your friends and family see you as a failure? Will they think you have more ambition than actual talent or perseverance? Our fear of being judged by others influences our behaviour more than we realise.

I often ask myself:

'If I were alone on an island, would I still jump off a cliff with a parachute?'

Or in other words:

'If I weren't on social media and told no one about it, would I still do what I do?'

Why do I do what I do? My answer is always:

'Because it makes me feel alive.'

Yet I can't deny that, to some extent, we all seek our place in society. We all want to be recognised for what we do. We chase status, even if it's just within a niche community of like-minded people.

No matter how individualistic you think you are, humans are inherently social beings. Belonging to a group increases your chances of survival—even though modern Western life is far removed from prehistoric struggles. We still crave acceptance and validation from our communities. So, ask yourself: why do you do what you do?

Would cyclist Remco Evenepoel still get on his bike if he had nothing left to win? Or if he had already won everything he ever wanted? In 2022, Dutch skater Kjeld Nuis became the fastest speed skater in history, reaching 103 km/h on ice. He is obsessed with his sport. In a podcast, he was asked:

'Will you keep skating once you stop competing at the Olympics?'

His answer?

'No, then I'll quit completely.'

That might sound extreme, but it makes sense. His drive is competition—being the fastest. Just skating for fun doesn't mean anything to him. Likewise, many professional footballers barely touch a ball again once they retire.

On the other hand, you have people like Kelly Slater, widely regarded as the GOAT of surfing. Even as he reaches the end of his career, he still competes among the top ten surfers in the world. And while he may soon retire, he'll never stop surfing—because the sport itself is his passion.

For me, why do I do what I do? It's a combination of recognition and personal joy. But I definitely didn't become a base jumper because my surroundings expected me to. If anything, they discouraged me from doing it. Unfortunately, many people let their environment dictate their life choices. Even in 2025, young people still follow the path their parents set for them.

Not long ago, I had a conversation with a 17-year-old boy.

'What are you going to study?' I asked.

'Medicine,' he replied. 'Everyone in my family is a doctor.'

'Do you actually want to do that?' I asked.

'No, but that's what they expect from me. My father would be really disappointed if I chose something else.'

From an early age, we are pressured to conform to social expectations. Some people spend their entire lives doing what others expect from them, prioritising pleasing their surroundings over following their own path.

I get it—going it alone is hard. We live in a society governed by norms and unwritten rules, and no one exists in isolation. But you have to find a balance. You don't have to reject society, but you should aim to participate on your own terms. Adapt without losing yourself. Fit in without fading into the crowd.

Without even realising it, that's the path I always followed. I carved my own way, but at the same time, I remained aware of my surroundings. My greatest fortune was that my parents never imposed specific expectations on me. My father was an entrepreneur, but I never felt pressured to follow in his footsteps or choose a particular career. They gave me the freedom to choose my own path. That's also how I raise my son—I want him to be free from the weight of my expectations.

Social expectations are like chains wrapped around your legs. They hold people back. I've lost count of how many people I've spoken to in the autumn of their lives, burdened with regret over abandoned dreams. 'I wanted to be a singer, but my parents didn't allow it,' one man told me. A woman dreamed of becoming a kindergarten teacher, but her parents forced her to train as a primary school teacher instead. Ironically, her younger sister was later allowed to pursue kindergarten teaching. A man with a deep passion for history longed to study at university, but his father intimidated him into choosing a 'safer' path—becoming a translator. He eventually ended up in banking, while his secret dream of opening a chocolate shop never came to life.

Parental expectations shape children in powerful ways—not just in our society, but everywhere, across all eras. Humans have always created rules and imposed social codes. But history is also filled with people who broke those rules and forged their own way. So—what will YOU do?

Social rules are part of human nature

Societal expectations play a much larger role in our lives than we sometimes realise. Every culture, community, and era has its own norms, yet some recurring themes shape individuals everywhere. Social expectations create peer pressure: even when a rule isn't legally enforced, we instinctively sense what our environment expects from us and adjust our behaviour accordingly.

The following themes appear worldwide:

- **Gender roles.** Every society expects individuals to behave according to specific gender norms. Traditionally, this means women act like women and men act like men—dictating their expression, interests, and career choices. Breaking free from these roles is challenging; the moment you step outside the lines, your surroundings push back.
- **Education and career choices.** Every society has prestigious fields of study and professions that hold more status than others. Some jobs are more socially accepted—think of the stereotypical difference between a surgeon and a garbage collector. When you deviate from the path your environment expects of you, you face resistance. Some parents even cut ties with children who choose their own way.
- **Relationships and marriage.** Social norms dictate when you should be in a relationship and when you should get married. A woman in her mid-30s without children is often asked, subtly but tactlessly, if she's considering starting a family. Those who wish to remain child-free (or have no choice in the matter) find themselves constantly having to explain. Society often expects people to follow a specific timeline, but many feel uncomfortable with such rigid expectations.
- **Self-image.** Beauty standards and expectations about how you present yourself can be incredibly demanding. If you stray from the norm, you will inevitably receive comments—often well-intended, yet carrying the implicit message that life would be easier if you conformed. These 'harmless' remarks can erode self-confidence and self-esteem. You can change your clothing style if you choose, but those whose bodies don't fit the ideal standard may struggle with mental health issues.

- **Parenting style.** Parenting styles change over time and across cultures, but in any society, straying from the norm invites (not-so-subtle) disapproval. In the past, a father was seen as weak if he didn't discipline his children with a slap. Today, that same slap is considered child abuse. The structure of families and the roles parents play in their children's lives are also bound by unspoken standards—fail to meet them, and you're labelled 'different.'
- **Cultural and religious norms.** Social expectations dictate how people engage with their cultural and religious identities. Your environment may pressure you into observing traditions that clash with your personal beliefs or values. This can include wearing a headscarf, getting married in a church, or baptising your children despite being non-religious yourself.
- **The influence of social media.** The rise of social media has created new expectations about how people present themselves online. Seeing curated posts from others can create pressure to adopt the same lifestyle—dictating everything from diet and travel destinations to fashion choices. Some people consciously avoid posting certain photos or opinions for fear of straying too far from what's deemed acceptable.
- **Success and achievements.** Society has various benchmarks for success, such as wealth, social status, and public recognition. Unconventional choices are often met with skepticism, regarded more as failures than as genuine success. In some circles, driving a luxury car is a status symbol. In others, it marks you as an environmental villain or a selfish materialist.
- **Expressing emotions.** Social norms even dictate how we express emotions. In some cultures, emotional restraint is valued—think of the British stiff upper lip. In others, like Italian culture, a lack of outward expression is seen as

suspicious. Straying from the norm can make you feel like an outsider.

For everything we do, expectations exist. Some choices are deemed acceptable, while deviating from the norm means breaking an unwritten social code. These social norms can be restrictive and change very slowly, yet throughout your life, you will encounter shifting expectations. Behaviours that are acceptable at one age suddenly become 'not done' as you grow older. Think of the harsh criticism women sometimes receive for wearing makeup past their fifties or the ridicule directed at men in their forties who take up an adventurous new hobby. By the time you hit 40, you're expected to own a house and preferably have started a family. Retiring too early is seen as odd, but working too long is just as questionable. And whatever you do, don't start acting 'crazy' once the first grey hairs appear—ageing is supposed to come with a certain dignity.

Remember: just be normal, that's already strange enough.

How social norms limit us

Social rules help maintain order and cohesion within a society, which is undeniably valuable. No one benefits from chaos or a society where everyone fends for themselves. At the same time, outdated social rules can stifle personal growth and prevent people from realising their full potential. There are several ways in which these ingrained norms become obstacles.

First, some expectations about behaviour can feel overly rigid. Why should you follow the path others have mapped out for you? Why shouldn't you be able to decide your own milestones and when to reach them? Strict rules limit your ability to explore the world and discover yourself. Social norms also imply that you must conform to a particular ideal. This creates pressure for some people—if they fail to fit the mould, they face judgement or even exclusion. This pressure to conform stifles creativity and discourages people from expressing their unique perspectives and talents, leading them to make choices that don't truly align with what they want.

Societal structures, such as the education system or the workplace, are not always equipped to support unconventional approaches—even when those approaches have the potential to succeed. This lack of support can prevent individuals from fully pursuing paths that align with their unique skills and ambitions.

Society also tends to enforce a narrow definition of success, typically equating it with financial wealth or professional status. People who do not fit this mould may feel they are not successful. But what if you've dedicated years of your life as a caregiver, ensuring a family member could live with dignity? Is that not also a form of success? A rigid definition of success leaves many people feeling undervalued or believing they have failed to fulfil their potential. Worse, it can create immense pressure to meet societal expectations, leading to a fear of failure or judgement. As a result, people hesitate to take risks or pursue unconventional paths—even though the most groundbreaking successes often come from doing exactly that.

Sometimes, it isn't even about what you do, but who you are. Some social norms perpetuate inequality and discrimination based on gender, race, or socioeconomic status. These systemic barriers make it harder for certain groups to access opportunities and fully develop their talents.

Social rules are not inherently bad. But some of them are outdated or rigid, making them suffocating for those who try to take a different approach. Others—such as bans on remote work—fail to keep pace with changing circumstances. Even worse than the rules themselves is our fear of breaking unwritten norms and inviting the judgement of others. In that case, you have to ask yourself:

Will I actually be judged, and if so, does it really matter? Is it truly that important that others approve of me?

Why we stay loyal to ingrained norms

Validation: that is why social norms are often so powerful. We crave acceptance from our surroundings to feel like part of the group. We want to be acknowledged and recognised. This search for approval is deeply ingrained in human nature. There are several reasons for this.

To begin with, humans are social beings. We long to be socially accepted. Back when we lived as nomadic hunter-gatherers, being cast out from the group meant certain death. That need for social acceptance is why we seek validation so strongly. We want to be acknowledged as members of our community. That is why compliments and recognition feel so good. Even being invited to group activities signals approval. When we receive this approval, we feel good. It strengthens social bonds.

However, the fear of exclusion can also push us to seek approval too desperately. Some people become anxious at the slightest bit of criticism and want reassurance that they still belong. This longing often manifests as people-pleasing: they do everything they can to gain others' approval. In such situations, they prioritise validation over their own values and thoughts. Instead of expressing themselves authentically, they do what others expect of them—or what they think others expect.

If you want to build genuine connections while staying true to yourself, you need to find a balance between social acceptance and authenticity. That balance isn't easy to strike because approval also shapes how we see and value ourselves. Recognition from others helps us view ourselves positively. It strengthens our belief in our abilities and strengths, contributing to a healthy self-image.

Negative feedback or a lack of validation can undermine our self-worth. It makes us doubt ourselves and feel like we are falling short. Social media plays a huge role in this dynamic. Many people seek approval online through likes, comments, and followers. This becomes a way of 'measuring' social value. Unfortunately, we also compare our numbers to those of others and draw conclusions about our worth. As if having more likes somehow makes us more valuable.

However, self-worth isn't only about how others see us. Self-awareness and a strong sense of identity also determine how we value ourselves. Yet, how others perceive us often influences how we identify. We all have our own beliefs, values, and interests, but when others recognise and validate them, we feel even more certain that our inner world matters. Unfortunately, this works both ways: when our environment does not appreciate certain aspects of who we are, it can lead to conflict—if not open conflict, then an inner struggle.

Having a different cultural background, gender identity, or religious belief can be enough to leave someone feeling excluded. Every society marginalises certain identities or beliefs. Some people form groups to advocate for social recognition, while others seek out safe spaces where they can be themselves without judgement or discrimination. But if you find no sense of belonging—neither in broader society nor in a community of like-minded individuals—it becomes difficult to face the world with a positive attitude.

In difficult times, we need validation more than ever. The reassurance that we are not imagining our problems or that we are not alone in our struggles offers emotional support. When you share your experiences or feelings with others, validation helps you feel understood and supported. That can be comforting. However, there is a difference between seeking emotional support and seeking validation to avoid uncomfortable emotions. Some people constantly need reassurance that they are still accepted, which is not healthy either.

In healthy relationships, there is mutual support and empathy. Both parties feel safe to share their thoughts and emotions. They support each other without judgement or conditions. But in unhealthy relationships, the need for validation often becomes an addiction. If you interpret every action of your partner as proof of love—or a lack thereof—your relationship may not be built to last.

Seeking validation in the workplace can be a way to ask for feedback and improve. When we present ideas, it feels good when others engage with them. Constructive feedback not only provides valuable insights but also makes us feel appreciated. Simply having your efforts acknowledged is motivating. However, needing validation to function is risky. Suppose you send a piece of writing for review and never receive any feedback—you may feel rejected. But is it really that bad? Not everyone handles feedback well either. We often struggle to accept criticism. But remember: there is a real difference between constructive criticism and being torn down. When you learn to appreciate feedback, it helps you grow both personally and professionally.

It is deeply human to seek validation and recognition from those around us. We are social beings, and evolutionarily, we have always needed to belong to a group—our survival once depended on it, and now our mental well-being does. Social bonds and group cohesion were essential for human survival and reproduction throughout history. Mutual recognition strengthened group identity and motivated everyone to contribute to the tribe. Those who were accepted and valued had access to food, protection, and the opportunity to have offspring. Approval from others indicated one's status within the group. Conversely, the fear of rejection was a real threat. Losing social status was, in effect, a threat to one's life. Exclusion made a person highly vulnerable to predators and drastically reduced their chances of reproduction.

Even in today's modern society, the need for approval persists, though in different forms and contexts. Social media is a high-tech translation of prehistoric group dynamics. We now seek validation through numbers and statistics, but the core remains the same: we want to be accepted and valued.

Although this drive for approval is deeply embedded in human nature, we do not have to be enslaved by it. You can live your own life and make your own choices. As human beings, we possess introspection, self-awareness, and autonomy. A healthy sense of self-worth and internal validation can coexist with a desire for connection with others. Confidence does not have to rely entirely on external validation.

Receiving recognition is gratifying, but who you are and what success means to you is ultimately more important than what others think. If social norms do not align with your personal values, conforming to them will not bring you happiness. Your values and priorities are, in essence, the only rules that truly matter. Yet, we remain so afraid of what others might think.

Opinions to fear

If you want to make authentic choices and take control of your own life, you must break free from the fear of what others think and say. The fear of other people's opinions—better known as FOPO—can become so overwhelming that it paralyses you. Sometimes, we are so preoccupied with how others perceive us that self-doubt and insecurity take over, making us hesitant to show who we truly are. In the era of social media, where outside judgement carries even more weight, social anxiety has become a real challenge.

FOPO, or social approval anxiety, can stem from various sources, such as childhood experiences or the way our brains are wired. From a young age, we crave approval from authority figures, such as parents and teachers. Positive reinforcement strengthens us, while criticism or rejection makes us feel ashamed or inadequate. These early experiences shape our self-image and influence how we believe others perceive us. Repeated rejection can later manifest as a persistent fear of being judged.

The fear of other people's opinions can deeply distort your self-image. It can affect your relationships, personal growth, and the decisions you make. Those who struggle with it tend to doubt themselves constantly and seek validation for every choice they make. This fear prevents you from taking risks and following your passion because you're afraid of being judged if something doesn't work out. In relationships, the fear of rejection can lead to a lack of intimacy and authenticity, making it difficult to openly discuss your feelings and desires. Opinion anxiety is often the driving force behind perfectionism, where people measure their achievements against unrealistic expectations—setting themselves up for failure every time. Social media only reinforces this dynamic, as your worth is measured in likes, comments, and followers. When everyone presents only an idealised version of their life, it can feel like you will never measure up. But perhaps you should be questioning the norm rather than yourself.

How to free yourself from FOPO

Overcoming the fear of others' opinions requires courage and resilience—sorry, but it won't be easy. Fortunately, there are techniques to help you gradually break free from it.

- The first step is self-awareness. What are your beliefs, thoughts, and habits? How do they relate to other people's opinions? Examine how you seek validation and why you do it. If you understand the root of your insecurity, you can start addressing it.

- Practice self-compassion. Be kind and understanding toward yourself, especially when facing criticism or rejection. Everyone doubts themselves at some point or feels vulnerable. It's okay to make mistakes and fall short of expectations. By forgiving yourself, you build resistance against self-criticism and develop a healthier inner dialogue.
- Clarify your values and priorities. Take time to reflect on what truly matters to you and what brings you fulfilment. This exercise will help you gain clarity, which, as I've explained before, acts as a compass for all your decisions and actions. Clarity allows you to stay true to yourself despite external pressure.
- Challenge cognitive distortions and limiting beliefs. To what extent do your thought patterns fuel your fear of others' opinions? Examples include black-and-white thinking, magical thinking, or catastrophising. Replace those negative thoughts with a more balanced and realistic perspective. Do you truly believe you are incapable of something? Or are you just afraid of what others will think? And is their opinion really that important?
- Set boundaries in your relationships and interactions to protect your emotional well-being and autonomy. Learn to say 'no' to requests or expectations that clash with your values or priorities. Surround yourself with people who support and respect your authenticity.
- While setting boundaries is essential, also push yourself to face situations that trigger your FOPO. Learn to express yourself authentically, even when it feels uncomfortable or uncertain. You'll find that the consequences are often far less disastrous than you feared. Sometimes, instead of judgement, you'll receive appreciation.
- Don't hesitate to seek support from friends, family, or even a therapist. Simply sharing what you're struggling

with can provide validation. It also offers new insights and encouragement, helping you overcome your fear of others' judgement.

When humanity still lived a nomadic existence, we had to put in effort to find food and shelter. But in today's world of abundance, we can satisfy nearly every desire instantly. Since effort is no longer necessary, we consistently choose immediate rewards. After all, why struggle when you don't have to?

The result is that we no longer fit into the very environment we created for ourselves. Our reward system is overstimulated to the point of being harmful. Not everyone is an addict, and certainly not to everything at once, but some people—due to their genetics, upbringing, or life circumstances—are more vulnerable to addiction and the lure of instant gratification.

6

Instant versus delayed gratification

Easy decisions
make your life harder,
hard decisions
make your life easier.

Our intellect is one of our most powerful assets, but our brains often sabotage us. Our brains crave rewards but instinctively avoid pain. As soon as something becomes too difficult or painful, we feel the urge to quit. After all, why put in effort if there is no reward in sight?

You can overcome this urge for instant gratification by learning to take pleasure in a task. That may sound terribly old-fashioned, and I don't want to come across as a pre-war fossil, but it is the truth. Unfortunately, it is a truth that seems to be fading away—now I really do sound like someone from the last century. Regretfully, I see a generation of young people who panic at the slightest conflict or setback. They no longer seem accustomed to dealing with difficult situations.

I certainly don't want to point fingers at young people, because their fragile resilience is not their fault. Instead, I look to my own generation. My belief is that exposure to resistance leads to greater resilience. Nowadays, children are excessively shielded from all possible dangers of the outside world. At the slightest ache or cough, they stay home from school, and their parents rush them to the doctor—often for nothing. Mums and dads look for a quick fix because they don't want their child to suffer any pain.

Of course, it is a good thing that parents care about their children. But as a parent, you can also make it clear: *Yes, it hurts for a moment, or you feel miserable right now, but soon the pain will lessen, and by tomorrow, you will likely feel much better.*

Just as parents shield their children, adults also try to protect themselves. Suppose you have depression—do you opt for antidepressants, or do you first try to change your lifestyle with healthier food, more exercise, and better sleep? Most people choose the convenience of a pill. My own mother takes medication for her high cholesterol, yet she still puts a jar of mayonnaise on the table. That's hardly consistent.

We are always seeking comfort. If we feel a little hungry, we immediately open the fridge. At the slightest hint of boredom, we pull out our smartphones to pass the time. Comfort feels—surprise!—comfortable, but in reality, it isn't. A life that is *too* comfortable appears to be linked to depression, anxiety, diabetes, and cardiovascular diseases.

Humans did not evolve to live in comfort. Our ancestors had no refrigerators—they had to hunt or gather berries when they were hungry. And they didn't even know if they would succeed in catching prey. But when they *did* manage to fill their stomachs, the reward was all the greater.

Our brains seek rewards while avoiding pain and discomfort, as this proved to be a successful survival tactic in the harsh wilderness. If you, as a prehistoric human, managed to secure high-calorie food, your day was a success—you had increased your chances of survival. Forming social bonds and being accepted as part of a group ensured protection and support.

The reward system in our brains encouraged this behaviour. Consuming high-calorie food triggered a surge of the neurotransmitter dopamine—a brief moment of intense happiness. Similarly, being embraced by the group made us feel good.

Our brains still function largely as they did tens of thousands of years ago. The problem is that our environment has changed drastically. The same neural pathways that once helped us survive in a hostile world now make us vulnerable to addictive substances and behaviours. Our reward system actually makes it harder to survive in an urban jungle where everything is readily available. Drugs, alcohol, high-calorie food, pornography, gambling—temptation lurks around every corner.

When humanity still lived a nomadic existence, we had to make an effort to find food and shelter. But in today's world of abundance, we can satisfy every desire instantly. The fact that we no longer *have* to exert effort means that we consistently choose immediate rewards. After all, why put in effort if you don't have to?

The conclusion is that we no longer fit the environment we *ourselves* have created. Our reward system is being stimulated so frequently that it has become harmful. Not everyone is addicted, of course, and certainly not to everything at once, but some people are unlucky enough to be genetically, socially, or circumstantially predisposed to falling victim to addiction and the lure of instant gratification.

The vast majority of the world's population doesn't drink alcohol, yet in the West, we have an unhealthy relationship with it. Here, alcohol is widely available, and we use it as a reward—whether after a stressful day at work or a long bike ride, a beer or a glass of wine is the go-to response. In fact, people often look at you strangely if you choose not to drink.

Despite that, I completely quit alcohol because I wanted to reset my brain's reward system. I constantly sought rewards—not necessarily in alcohol, but in everything. At six in the morning, the first thing my body craved was coffee! It was as if I had to reward myself all day long, like I was training my own pet. It didn't feel right—I was caught in an unhealthy dopamine cycle. My reward centre was so overstimulated that I was constantly seeking instant gratification: a piece of candy here, scrolling through reels on my phone there, and then finishing the day with a glass of wine. That's why I chose a hard reset: I cut out the 'biggest' reward—alcohol.

If you don't gain control over your reward system, you leave yourself vulnerable to addiction. It could be social media, food, porn, or drugs—anything that gives an immediate dopamine hit. And once you're addicted, you need more to reach the same level of satisfaction.

What's the first thing you do when you wake up? For many people, it's grabbing their phone and checking messages and notifications. It seems harmless, but it's not. You're starting your day by immediately chasing instant gratification.

Thanks to modern technology and comfort, we have direct access to an endless stream of stimuli. The internet, social media, fast food, and online shopping ensure that we never have to wait long to get what we want. The challenge is no longer working to obtain something—the real challenge is resisting all these temptations. For people with an impulsive nature, this is especially difficult. Even if you know that compulsive shopping or substance use isn't healthy, your brain doesn't exactly help you change your behaviour.

Our lives have become a constant chain of fleeting pleasures. Imagine you've been dreaming of a new car—your favourite brand, the exact model you've always wanted. Finally, you manage to buy it. It feels incredible! The first few weeks, every drive fills you with joy. But after a few months, you realise you're not actually happier—no matter how much you enjoy driving it. You start craving another thrill. Maybe it's time for a new racing bike?

Compulsive shopping is just another addiction driven by a disrupted reward system. The ease of online shopping makes it even worse—many people try to curb their spending by returning their purchases, but the ability to return items only reinforces their addiction.

In my view, the urge for instant gratification is strongest in people who have too much time to think and lack real challenges. They chase comfort in small pleasures, yet true happiness remains elusive. But I do believe happiness exists. And now, you're probably wondering: What actually makes people happy? I think the answer is this: the feeling that you're giving your own life meaning.

Hard-earned happiness lasts longer

The key to happiness is ensuring you can take care of yourself and find solutions when needed. Psychology has a term for this: self-efficacy, or self-reliance. It refers to your confidence in your ability to successfully influence your environment—whether by completing a task, solving a problem, or navigating challenges. This is not the same as self-confidence. Self-efficacy is specifically the belief that you can solve problems in any environment.

If you grew up in the 1980s, you might immediately think of MacGyver. He could get out of any tricky situation by coming up with ingenious solutions. But self-efficacy goes far beyond that—it also involves overcoming mental and social obstacles. It's about being prepared, knowing that you can always learn something new, and understanding that past experiences equip you to handle future problems. That knowledge alone is incredibly empowering.

That brings us to real happiness, which lies more in delayed gratification. While those chasing instant gratification rely on quick, easy bursts of satisfaction, delayed gratification requires you to step out of your comfort zone and push your boundaries. This can apply to almost anything in life. But the payoff is immense.

Many people seem to believe that happiness means eliminating all difficulties or anything unpleasant from life. But humans didn't evolve in a perfect world—far from it. For millennia, we have lived in a world full of challenges and dangers. That's what our brains expect. Even if we remove all threats from our immediate surroundings, our minds will still seek them out. This can lead to anxiety disorders, where the body suddenly enters a state of panic for no apparent reason. For some people, even ordinary daily situations trigger this reaction. The instinctive response is to avoid the things that cause fear. But as you might have guessed, avoidance only makes the fear grow stronger. It's not the actual dangers that make us anxious—it's our tendency to avoid them. Exposure to what frightens us, no matter how unpleasant, is far more effective in the long run.

As contradictory as it sounds, we need discomfort to feel truly happy. When we overcome real challenges, we don't just experience satisfaction—we gain a profound sense of fulfilment: the knowledge that we belong in this world and that we are capable of handling its obstacles. The most intense moments in your life were likely the ones where you were tested the hardest. The greatest happiness comes from enduring a difficult journey and seeing it through to the end.

This is precisely why having a child is such an unforgettable moment of joy. Getting pregnant isn't always easy, and then come nine months of uncertainty: Will everything go well? Are we ready for this? How will our lives change? Women carry a physical burden, but pregnancy is a challenge for both parents. And then comes the climax—the birth itself. After all these challenges, holding their baby for the first time is a powerful example of delayed gratification.

Be honest—if you grab a tub of Biscoff ice cream from the freezer, you're not going to say, ten years from now, 'That was one of the most intense moments of my life—I'll never forget that ice cream!' Without struggle, there is no deep happiness—that's the essence of delayed gratification. Take it from me: writing a book is an uncomfortable process. It takes a long time, it's difficult, and you know that once it's finished, people will judge it. Even after all your hard work, there's no guarantee it will be successful or find an audience. And yet—when you finally open that box and hold your book in your hands for the first time, flipping through its pages, the satisfaction is unparalleled. Even years later, you'll still feel proud: Damn, I wrote a book!

A friend of mine is a rollerblader and saw a girl at a skate park trying to roll down a ramp into the bowl. On her first attempt, she fell on her backside. She started crying and refused to try again. But fifteen minutes later, she reappeared at the edge of the bowl. The rollerblader offered to help her. 'I know how to hold your arm so that you won't fall, no matter what,' he said. 'No pressure, but if you're ready, I'd love to help you.' A few minutes later, the girl made a second attempt. Successfully! She screamed with joy, throwing her clenched fists in the air. That, too, is delayed gratification. She had already experienced how painful failure can be. Rolling down a steep edge is far outside your comfort zone if you've never done it before. But she really wanted to be able to do it. She took the leap, and she will never forget how happy she was in that moment.

I, myself, am now used to delayed gratification because my entire sport is built on discomfort. Every jump requires effort and preparation. You work towards that one moment. Every jump carries a significant risk, and it's always difficult to take that step and actually make the jump. But the sense of accomplishment is immense. That is something completely different from opening the candy cupboard and putting something sweet in your mouth.

When I was about to make my first base jump, the threshold was enormous. There I was, standing on a bridge at the border with Germany. Mentally, physically, and in terms of equipment, I was completely ready. As an experienced skydiver, I also knew what falling felt like. And yet, I was about to take a step into the unknown. That moment was so intense that I can still remember the scent of the forest. The sounds of nature. It felt terribly uncomfortable. And then I jumped. That's something you remember for the rest of your life. My physical and mental discomfort was replaced by immense satisfaction.

Another example is fitness. People often ask me, 'What do you do to stay in shape?' The answer is: I go down to my cellar. In that bare concrete space, I have my spinning bike. I sit there and pedal for an hour. I can assure you: that is anything *but* instant gratification.

'Impossible! I wouldn't do that,' people say when they hear that. 'Do you think *I* enjoy it?' I ask them. 'Do you think I get up and, for fun, go sweat for an hour in my cellar?'

'Uh, no...' Then they have no idea why I voluntarily go down to my cellar every morning. 'At the moment you start, it's not fun, but the reward afterward, in my mind, is insane.'

I also regularly take ice baths, even though I really don't like them. In fact, I *hate* them. And yet, I do it, because the dopamine rush is amazing. It also lasts much longer than when you eat dessert or drink a glass of wine. That's just the power of delayed gratification. And on top of that, you feel like you've accomplished something difficult or overcome a challenge. *I did it!*

Ultra-runners and mountaineers also know the feeling of delayed gratification. Their sport is painful and even dangerous, but the reward when they reach the finish line or the summit is something they will never forget.

Discipline in a world full of temptations

Rigid social norms frustrate me—they keep people in line and stop them from chasing their dreams. But there are some old-fashioned norms that, in my opinion, deserve a comeback. One of them is self-discipline. These days, lasting happiness takes self-discipline. We live in a world full of temptation and comfort. That means you need discipline to resist instant gratification so that you can experience the deeper joy of delayed gratification.

In the West, we have the luxury of comfort at our fingertips. In the past, people had no choice—they had to wash themselves with cold water. But today, steaming hot water flows instantly from the showerhead. If you want that dopamine kick from an icy blast, you have to make a deliberate choice to turn your thermostat down.

Supermarket shelves are overflowing with sugary, fatty foods that contain little to no nutrients. Water takes up only a tiny corner of the soft drinks aisle. The wine section is often the most beautifully decorated part of the store, making it all the more tempting. As a result, making healthy choices requires effort—so much effort that a vast number of people struggle with excess weight. And because we want everyone to feel good about themselves, we've normalised obesity. I don't judge people for their weight, but I do question whether they truly feel good in their bodies when they are overweight. Every single study shows that, in the long run, excess weight is unhealthy and leads to a whole range of lifestyle diseases.

Our unhealthy lifestyle has unfortunately become the new normal, even in athletic families. I recently watched a documentary about a Belgian family of elite athletes who are also in the horse-breeding business. What was on their breakfast table? Hazelnut spread, breakfast cereals, and bottles of fruit juice. Those products are pure sugar. I was genuinely shocked. Normally, top athletes are very conscious of their diet, yet here they were, feeding their own children—children they hope will also become champions—sugar from day one.

I know I would have a problem if I started getting a belly. It's like the old 'frog in boiling water' metaphor: you don't notice the temperature rising until it's too late. Unfortunately, sugary temptations are everywhere, and in our culture, it's frowned upon to deprive yourself of anything.

Once a sign of wealth, excess weight, is now common across all social classes due to the easy availability of calorie-dense food. I'll admit—I'm addicted to sugar, too. I love hazelnut spread. But I firmly believe that one day, those products will be banned from store shelves because they're just too unhealthy. The mere fact that they're available fuels addiction because, as humans, we can't resist them. Psychological studies show the same thing: we always choose the quick reward.

A famous experiment illustrates this perfectly. Researchers asked children: 'Would you rather have one cookie now or two cookies tomorrow?' The rational answer is, 'I'll take two tomorrow.' But nearly all of them took the one cookie right away. They simply couldn't resist the immediate temptation. And that's not just because they're children—rational adults fall into the same trap. The certainty of a reward now is much stronger than the promise of a possible reward later. That's how deeply wired our brains are for instant gratification.

The only solution is to become aware of this mechanism and learn to make conscious choices. Every now and then, I do choose sugar, whether in food or an energy drink—if I have a physically demanding challenge ahead of me. If you don't have enough sugar in your system at those moments, you crash and end up consuming even more sugar later. But in our comfortable Western lifestyle, we consume far too much sugar. We don't need that extra energy—quite the opposite. Yet, those sweet temptations keep triggering our cravings at full force.

Since I quit alcohol, the temptation of sugar has only grown stronger. If I'm not careful, I could devour twenty Biscoff cookies in one go. Mmm, just writing about it makes me crave them. That's my weak spot, and I have to make a real effort to resist the temptation. But here's the fascinating part: resisting that urge actually gives me more satisfaction than eating those twenty cookies. People who give in to their gluttony often regret it afterward. You feel bloated and uncomfortable. The short-lived pleasure of a greasy burger doesn't bring deeper satisfaction—it just leaves discomfort in its wake.

In that sense, I find intermittent fasting interesting: it's an exercise in resisting temptation while also keeping your metabolism flexible. Intuitive eating is another compelling concept. It involves making conscious choices about whether to eat and what to eat. I try to be very deliberate about those choices—if something isn't healthy, I leave it alone. I've even trained myself not to eat if I can't find anything nutritious. That way, I gain control over my cravings.

The added bonus is that self-discipline itself can become addictive. Denying yourself cheap temptations boosts your self-confidence and even happiness. You often hear this from people who have quit drinking: the drive to stay sober becomes stronger than the desire for alcohol. If you crave clarity and control, alcohol's intoxicating effect can even feel like an annoyance. (Unfortunately, I still feel perfectly clear-headed after wolfing down twenty Biscoff cookies.)

I'm lucky to be a morning person. As soon as I'm out of bed, I want to start my day—that alone gives me an immediate sense of satisfaction. If you wake up at five or six in the morning, there are fewer distractions. And when you wake up naturally, you feel much sharper than when an alarm jolts you out of sleep.

Then, I head to my cellar for an hour of spinning. The reward I give myself isn't a bowl of Biscoff cookies, but a brain flooded with dopamine. That's precisely why I can convince myself every morning to push my body to the limit. It's not an addiction—I have to work for that dopamine rush—but it brings me immense satisfaction.

Where do addictions come from?

The brain's reward system runs on neurotransmitters like dopamine. Whenever we have a positive experience, dopamine is released, making us feel good for a moment. Over time, our brain starts associating certain stimuli with that dopamine rush, making us actively seek them out. Substances like drugs and alcohol, but also gambling and calorie-dense foods, trigger that reward system. And you can guess the consequence: once we've felt the pleasure of that reward, we want more. Since our brain adapts to dopamine spikes, we need increasingly larger doses to feel the same level of reward. Eventually, a habit turns into a pattern of addiction.

Some people are unlucky and are genetically more prone to addiction. If your reward system reacts strongly to stimuli, you have a higher risk of developing dependencies on certain substances or behaviours. Environmental factors like stress or social surroundings can also push bad habits into full-blown addictions. Because of the interaction between genetics and environment, addiction is an extremely complex phenomenon.

But I also notice a recurring pattern. I see addictions—whether to sugar, porn, or alcohol—as a disconnection from yourself. You've lost touch with who you are and what really matters. People who are deeply connected to themselves and live with intention tend to notice much sooner when they're on the brink of addiction.

Many addictions don't arise out of nowhere—they stem from the desire to fill an inner void, soothe emotional needs, or process unresolved trauma. People struggling with addiction often have difficulty managing their emotions. Their addiction is an attempt to calm or escape painful feelings such as anxiety, depression, or loneliness. Those who are unable to process their emotions in a healthy way are more vulnerable to addiction. A lack of self-awareness or self-acceptance often plays a role as well. If you don't have a clear sense of who you are and what your purpose is, you're at greater risk of addiction. The dopamine rush becomes your way of finding meaning and stability, but it's an illusion of belonging. In reality, you drift even further from who you truly are and what you're capable of.

If you didn't experience secure attachment as a child and struggle with social connections as a result, building healthy relationships can be extremely difficult. Social isolation often leads to addiction, and addiction, in turn, deepens that isolation. Healthy relationships and a supportive environment are crucial for our well-being, but when they're absent, we start seeking other ways to escape loneliness.

Societal factors such as poverty and discrimination also open the door to addiction. In a fair and healthy society, there is less need for intoxication as a means of escape.

Even in rats, this mechanism has been demonstrated. In Bruce Alexander's Rat Park experiments, rats in a stimulating and social environment were far less likely to consume morphine than those kept in isolated, unstimulating cages. Johann Hari made a similar argument in his book Chasing the Scream (2015), stating that the opposite of addiction isn't sobriety—it's connection. He emphasised that building meaningful relationships and finding a place in society are essential to preventing or overcoming addiction.

Addiction isn't solved simply by forcing people to abandon their addictive behaviours. You also have to help them rebuild or strengthen their social bonds. And just as importantly, they must learn that delaying gratification is worthwhile—often, the longest road to fulfilment is the healthiest one.

Connect with yourself

Fulfilment—whether immediate or delayed—always stems from something you've done or experienced. But there's an even deeper form of happiness: a connection with yourself. The feeling of being in alignment with who you are and well-adapted to the world around you—that is where true happiness lies. It forms a solid foundation to build upon. When that connection exists, you are far less likely to fall into temptation.

In everything I've done and continue to do, I have sought ways to grow as a person. That drive has always fascinated me, no matter how difficult the journey was at times. I was never fixated on end results but rather on my personal development. Because I have a solid inner core, I've had the courage to step outside my comfort zone.

People often ask me if I set big goals for myself. The answer is no, not really. I never have. A goal is useless if you don't enjoy the journey toward it. For me, the process of improving every day is more satisfying than actually reaching a goal. Even if you don't achieve a goal, the journey itself can still be valuable. With that mindset, you stay connected to yourself and are less likely to get caught in the web of addiction. The satisfaction comes from within, from what you do—not from consuming or buying things. Only when you lose that connection with yourself do you start looking for external sources of fulfilment.

That might sound like I'm a Buddhist at heart, but trust me—I'm far from zen. On the contrary—I get frustrated very quickly when something doesn't work out. I want to be good at what I do. But I'm no longer 20, and I don't always remember that. When things don't move fast enough for my liking, I have to hit the pause button: Wait, you're trying to rush this. You're trying too hard to prove yourself. Because I want to see results quickly, I can be too hard on myself. At least I'm aware of it.

A few years ago, I started playing padel. As a kid, I played a bit of tennis, and as a student, I played a lot of squash, so racket sports weren't unfamiliar to me. But I didn't want to just be a casual player. I trained and trained to get as good as possible. If I could have, I would've practiced at night to improve my level.

The desire to improve every day sometimes leads to frustration. Even achieving micro-goals can disrupt your connection with yourself. That's when you have to remind yourself: it's not about the skills you gain; it's about growing as a person.

I've become better at that over time. Ten years ago, I was more intense whenever I took on something new—I had to reach the top. Now, it's more about having fun and staying curious. Still, I set the bar high. That's not always healthy, but you can push yourself without becoming frustrated.

Let's go back to my cellar. Yes, I have to push myself to walk down the stairs and get on my spinning bike. But once I find my rhythm, I actually enjoy the struggle. My heart rate spikes as I work through my high-intensity interval training. It's explosive—an intensity I don't often experience elsewhere. I don't sweat easily, but I do during these sessions. And I love it. My music is blasting, and I reach a kind of euphoria. The feeling is comparable to having a few glasses of wine.

After every session, I feel on top of the world. Knowing that helps me get on that bike in the first place. I'm also working toward a long-term goal: improving my VO_2 max, my maximum oxygen uptake capacity. VO_2 max and muscle mass are the two biggest longevity markers—they determine how healthy you are and how long you'll live.

I'm 52 years old. If I can do everything I want for another fifteen years, that's great, but really, only fifteen years?! That's nothing. So, I want to keep doing as much as possible for as long as possible. That means I do have a goal. My VO_2 max is currently at 47, which is already very high for my age, but I want to push it to 50. Then I'll know: Cedric, you've got a long way to go. That's another reason I look forward to my spinning sessions. There's the release at the end—the delayed gratification—but there's also the bigger picture: my health. It feels good knowing I'm keeping my body in top condition, delaying or minimising the effects of ageing. This morning at 8 AM, as I was spinning, I felt euphoric when I saw my VO_2 max had gone up again.

Now, you could say, 'Pff, we all die anyway, why not just go to a burger joint?' And yes, that's true—we all die. But not in the same way. The biggest regret among older people isn't what they didn't do—that used to be common. Nowadays, their biggest regret is that they should have taken better care of their health because, for the last fifteen years of their lives, they could only sit in a chair. And it could have been different if they had lived more healthily. That's why I get so much satisfaction from making sure now that I'll still be healthy and physically capable later.

Looking for certainty is the best and fastest way to give up on your dreams.

Conclusion

Gain control by letting go of control

There are many things we take for granted, as if they will always remain the same. Take peace, for example. Most people in Western Europe have never experienced war, making it seem absurd to think that our peaceful existence could ever come to an end. Yet the world is a cruel and chaotic place. Sooner or later, war will find its way here, perhaps sooner than we'd like to believe. We are living in highly uncertain times. The war in Ukraine is shaking Europe to its core, the Middle East is in flames, and the rivalry between China and the United States is unpredictable.

How do you deal with that uncertainty? Consistency is the answer. COVID, the energy crisis, and ongoing wars have reminded us that the world is chaotic and unpredictable. Uncertainty is the only certainty. Unpredictability is the natural order of things. For decades, we in the West lived with blinders on, but the world has always been chaotic, and it remains so. Our comfortable lives gave us a false sense of security. (And we weren't even happy because of it—quite the opposite.)

Humans always want to be in control, yet the news reminds us daily that we control almost nothing. Even the most ruthless dictators fail to bend reality to their will. Despite torture camps and arsenals capable of wiping out the planet, things rarely go exactly as they want. For the average citizen, the news is even more unsettling: you are a pawn in a game played by higher powers, at the mercy of a fickle fate. Dangerous viruses and energy crises dominate the headlines, but even your daily commute remains a potential hazard. And you never know when a drunk driver might cross your path.

Our brains are wired to focus on potential threats. We feel the urge to retreat into the bunker that our homes have become. But even there, we can't keep all danger at bay. Constantly seeking comfort and security does not make us happy. Some people try to control their lives by eliminating every possible risk. But new risks always emerge, forcing them into a never-ending battle to maintain control. The result? They only become more fearful.

Control is an illusion. In reality, you can control almost nothing. The only thing you can control is how you respond to uncertainty—how you behave, how you perceive reality. It's not what happens, but how you frame it. Keep what is within your control in check, and let go of the rest. Real control is about setting your own course and knowing that you have the ability to adapt to changing circumstances. Here's the paradox: by letting go of control and embracing the unexpected, you actually gain a sense of control. Because you know: I am prepared. No matter what happens, I will adapt and handle it.

On the other hand, if you try to eliminate all risks or rely on others to solve your problems, then your illusion of control is actually a symptom of fear and insecurity. Fear is not the solution. Many people see uncertainty as a problem. I see it as a tool—one that forces me to keep learning. Uncertainty keeps me sharp.

Certainty bores me. Predictability puts me to sleep. The constant search for security is the surest way to abandon your dreams. A healthy dose of uncertainty is a powerful way to challenge yourself, reinvent yourself, and stay relevant. The awareness that everything could end tomorrow keeps you awake. This is not about fear—it's about awareness, even acceptance. The future is uncertain, so I must live now.

Don't lock yourself away in your cave or your comfortable bunker—go out and hunt, gather food. If you hide, you won't eat, and you'll starve. If you go searching for food, you risk encountering a predator and dying. But if you stay alert, chances are you'll find food and survive another day. So: we go for it. We commit. Athletes must accept that they can't control everything. You prepare as well as you can, and then you have to let go. It's only by taking action that you discover yourself and know where you stand.

It's human nature to want to plan and control everything, but ultimately, this is just a way to deny death. When you book a vacation for Christmas or the summer, your brain assumes: I'll still be here by then. Because you've planned something, you feel like you have a grip on the future. But the future doesn't bend to your plans, and the more you try to control it, the more you lose control over the present. Focus too much on the future, and the present slips through your fingers. Don't fall into that trap—it will only make you unhappy.

My rule of thumb is to bet everything on the now. The past is fixed, the future is untouchable, but the now is yours to shape. By focusing solely on the now, you actually gain far more control over the future than by making endless plans. This is especially true in dangerous situations—being grounded in the moment is the only thing you can control. If you lose sight of the now in such a situation, you simply won't have much of a future left.

Let's change our perception of uncertainty. Say you have an idea to open a new store in an industry you know well. My response? That's amazing, that's your passion. It's a niche market, but you understand the business. Someone else might say: That market is too small, it won't work, and there's so much paperwork involved. Often, it's parents who react this way—trying to 'protect' their children from failure.

And when someone does take the leap and fails, some people have the audacity to say: See? I knew it. I told you so. That attitude infuriates me. It goes against everything I believe in. Instead of praising someone for their courage and effort, you push them even further down. A negative mindset like that genuinely makes me angry. At best, these comments are a projection of the speaker's own fear of failure. At worst, they're rooted in jealousy or frustration.

Some cyclists are furious at people who don't wear helmets—not just professional riders, but casual cyclists too. They accuse helmetless riders of being irresponsible or even stupid. But these 'helmet activists' believe in a lie: a helmet is no guarantee against injury. It's primarily a way to create an illusion of control over uncertainty. Letting go of that need for control can be incredibly liberating. You'll have to cycle more attentively, but you take your fate into your own hands.

I'm always aware of how little I actually control. I can't influence what other people do. But I can control my reaction. And by this, I don't mean 'controlling' my emotions—because that, too, is an illusion. Most of the time, 'controlling' emotions just means ignoring, suppressing, or denying them. But emotions exist, and sooner or later, they'll surface—often more intensely than before. Say you're frustrated but refuse to admit it. You tell yourself: No, I have no reason to be frustrated. Everything's fine. Meanwhile, that frustration festers inside you, eventually leading to burnout, depression, or explosive anger. The real question is not whether you feel an emotion, but what you do with it. Denying frustration is a form of toxic positivity—something that annoys me just as much as a negative mindset. Blindly insisting that everything is fine is just another attempt to control your environment. Having the courage to say things are not okay actually takes far more strength and will get you much further. That's a far healthier mindset than pretending challenges don't exist.

In uncertain times, you're backed into a corner and forced to make choices. It's uncomfortable, but also a powerful catalyst for growth. Uncertainty challenges you to develop new skills, solve problems, and adapt. Learning to navigate uncertainty makes you more creative and emotionally intelligent. Those who embrace it rather than fear it are the ones who achieve their dreams. They strive to become so good at what they do that they become indispensable—gaining more control over their lives in the process.

Mastery brings a deep sense of fulfilment. It's the best defense against crisis and chaos. When you know you're good at something, you can weather any storm. A writer might worry that in two years, AI will overtake the market. But if you're truly great at your craft, you'll keep evolving—and no algorithm will ever replace you. Keep refining your talents, learn new skills, and challenge yourself. Never stop growing.

Passing that mindset onto children prepares them for an uncertain future. Are we putting too much pressure on them? No—the real danger lies in making them afraid. Worse still, in misleading them into thinking that everything will magically work out. If they suddenly face setbacks, they won't know how to handle them.

What we shouldn't demand from children is perfection—that breeds fear and uncertainty. Instead, we should foster curiosity, encourage them to try, fail, and try again. Reward effort, not just results. Show them that after a difficult journey comes an immense mental reward: the pride of having achieved something, the growth that comes with it, and the sense of connection with oneself. Shielding children from uncertainty only makes them fragile. Exposing them to it forces them to adapt and find solutions. That, in turn, sharpens their cognitive agility.

Time and again, uncertainty has fueled creativity and innovation. When the world is shaken up, we become more open to questioning old norms and trying new approaches. When our beliefs no longer seem to hold up, we have no choice but to adopt a growth mindset. Rather than seeing uncertainty as a threat, we can recognise it as an opportunity for personal growth. With a growth mindset, we stay open to new possibilities, learn from failures, and constantly strive for self-improvement.

So don't let fear, limiting beliefs, or rigid social norms hold you back. Don't shy away from the long, difficult road. If you know what matters to you and you're willing to take responsibility for your own path, you're ready to rise above yourself. Let go of comfort. Chase your dreams.

Acknowledgments

Thanks to my family and friends who have always supported me, but also to the 'Red Bull' family, who have been giving me wings and energy for 25 years to make my dreams come true and push my limits.

Literature

- *The Subtle Art of Not Giving a F*ck* — Mark Manson
- *Beyond Good and Evil* — Friedrich Nietzsche
- *The Daily Stoic* — Ryan Holiday
- *Meditations* — Marcus Aurelius
- *Finding Your Element* — Ken Robinson